SMART SKETCH BOOK 4

Oogie Art's step-by-step guide to painting still life objects in acrylic.

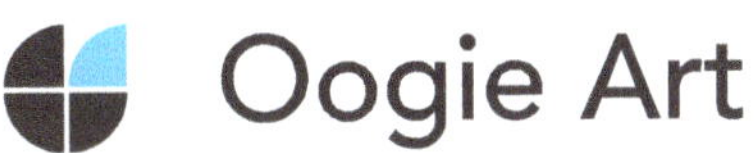

Oogie Art's SmartSketchbook™
An Expert's Guide to Still Life in Acrylic
First Edition, Copyright © 2015

Produced and Edited by
Oogie Art
New York, NY

© Text
Oogie Art

© Photographs
Licensed under Oogie Art®

Directed by
Wook Choi

Assistant Directed by
Clara Lu

Drawings by
Jee Hwang

Tips by
Wook Choi

Published and Distributed by
Oogie Publishing House
New York, NY
www.oogiepublishinghouse.com
(212) 714-1011

ISBN 978-0-9855809-5-7
Printed in the United States

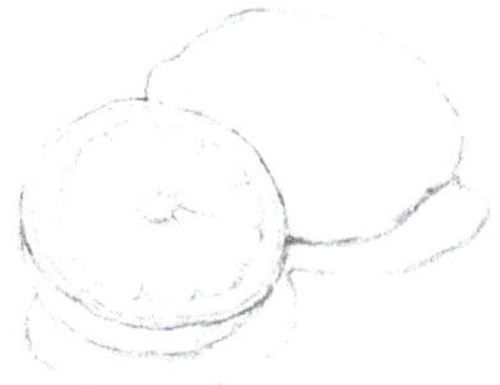 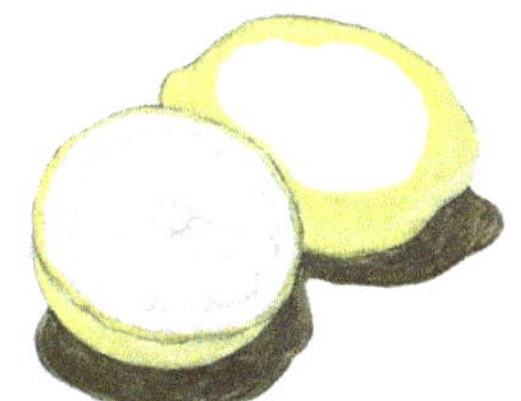 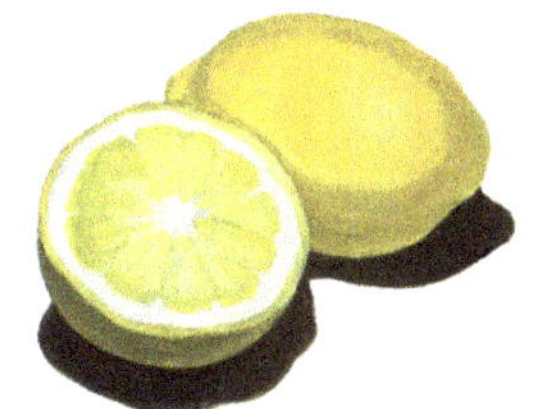 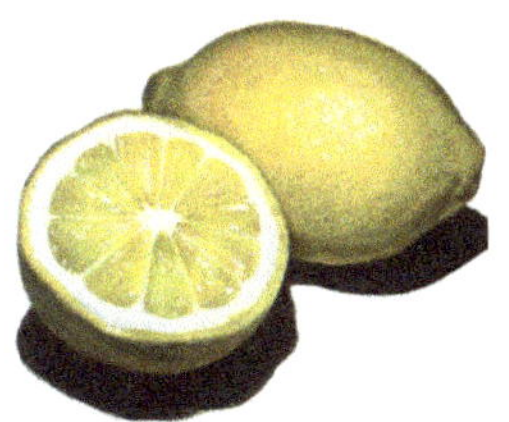

CONTENTS

Introduction to Acrylic Paint

Acrylics make a great first foray into painting. These paints are a safer alternative to oil paints and provide a good introduction to value, color, mixing paint, and brushwork without having to worry about extra chemicals and solvents. Plus, because of its strong adhesion, acrylic paint will not crack no matter how thick the layers are. Acrylic paints can mimic the quality of oil paints. When thinned with a lot of water, acrylics can also mimic the qualities of watercolor. Acrylics are water-based and tend to dry fairly quickly (sometimes in a matter of minutes), so you will need to wash your brushes immediately after each session. To avoid waste, use only as much paint as you think you would need for your painting session, you can always add more when you need it.

Start with a set of 12 to 18 colors of the rainbow, then add on more colors as you paint more with acrylic. Always have a large tube of Titanium white.

What you'll need

- Brushes (an assortment Bright and Round brushes in varying sizes), refer to page 6 for guidance
- Acrylic Paints in varying colors
- Paper Palette
- Palette Knife
- Canvas

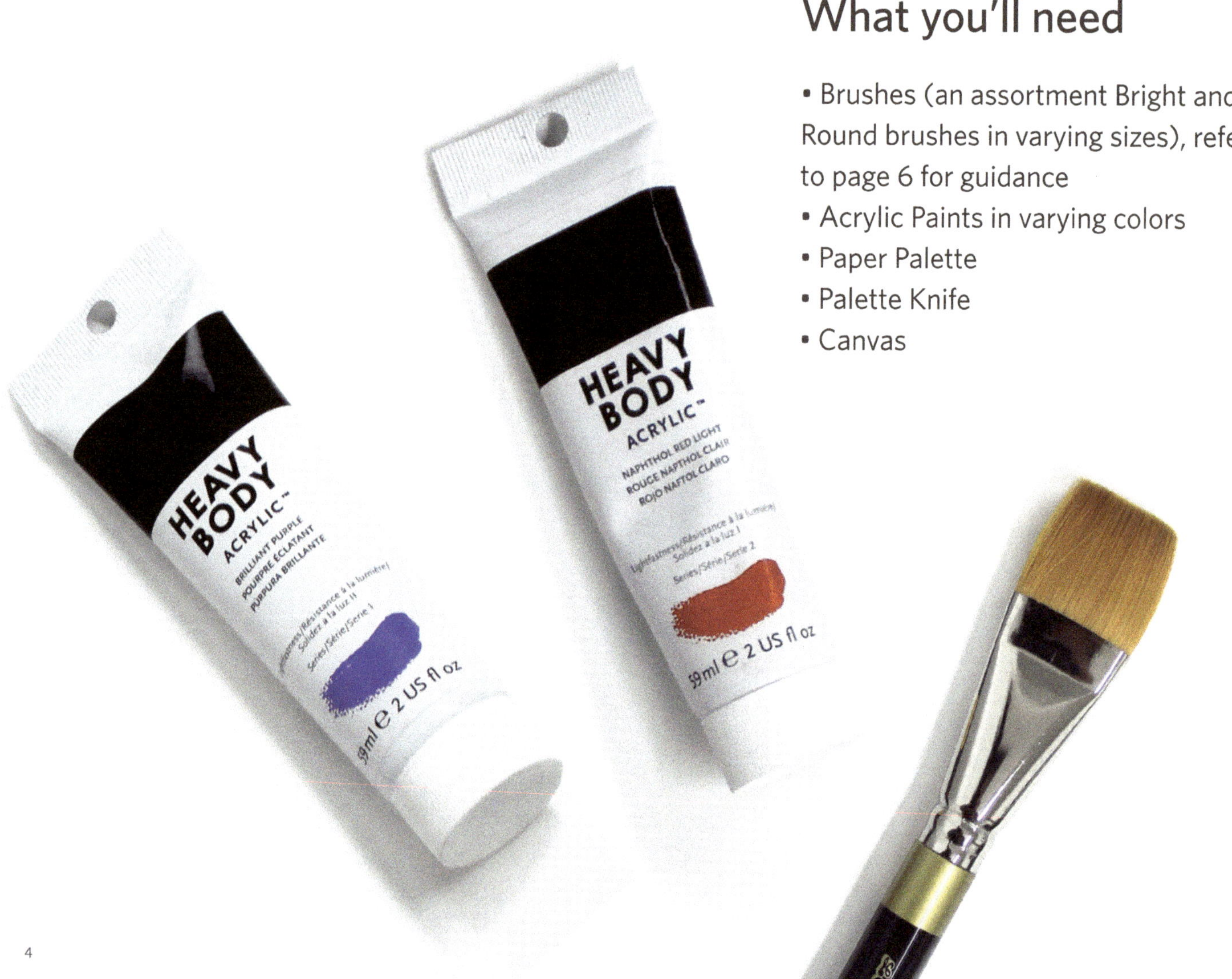

Types of Acrylic Paint

Acrylic paints come in varying thicknesses with their own distinct advantages and disadvantages. Low-priced acrylic paints are ideal for painting large areas, concealing brush strokes, and fine details. Other acrylic paints are great for thick impasto work, retaining brush textures, and blending due to their longer drying time.

Types of White and Black Acrylic Paint

The difference between Zinc white and Titanium white is transparency. Zinc white is more transparent than titanium white, a quality that is useful when adjusting skin tones without making colors too "chalky."

A similar difference exists between Ivory and Mars black. Mars black is much more opaque (although not as black as Ivory black) and is much stronger when mixing with color.

Acrylic Medium

Acrylic mediums are generally used to extend paints and modify the transparency of your colors. A liquid medium will also make your paints less viscous and easier to manipulate, making them ideal for fine details. Heavy body medium is used for thick impasto techniques as well as extending colors.

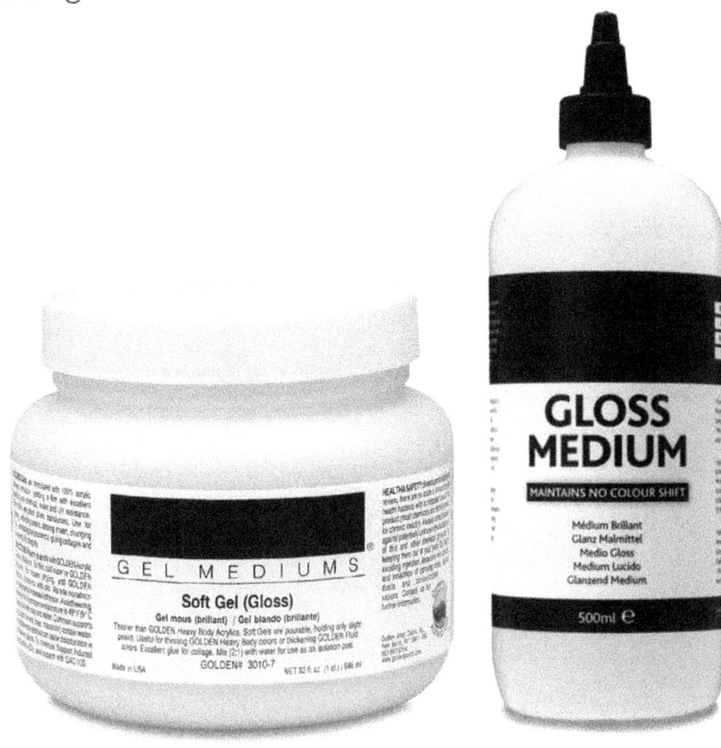

Types of Paintbrush Fibers

The world of brushes can become very complicated as preferences for brush type and shape differ from artist to artist. In general, here are some guidelines when choosing brushes.

The hair that makes up the brush is very important to how it handles paint. In general, brushes designed for acrylic paints tend to work well with other types, especially oil, while brushes designed for oil and watercolor tend to dry out and become brittle with acrylics. Brushes come in a variety of natural and synthetic fibers.

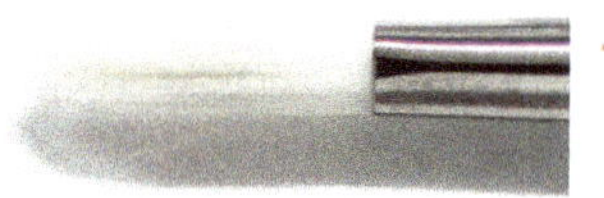

Sable - These brushes are made from natural soft hair of a weasel. They are best for watercolor and oil painting and hold a fine point or edge.

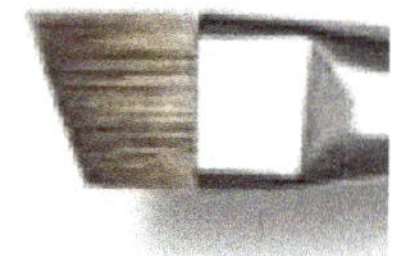

Mongoose - These brushes make a great alternative to sable-hair brushes, which are more expensive. They are slightly stiffer than sable brushes, are very versatile, and make a great option for acrylic, oil, and watercolor.

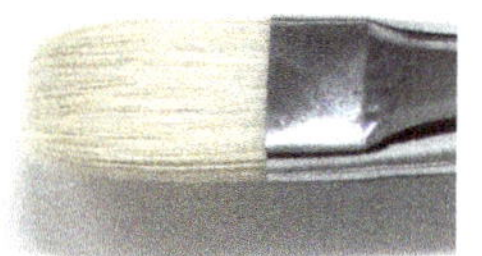

Bristle - Bristle brushes are much stiffer than other natural hairs. These brushes are great for spreading oil and acrylic paint smoothly and evenly.

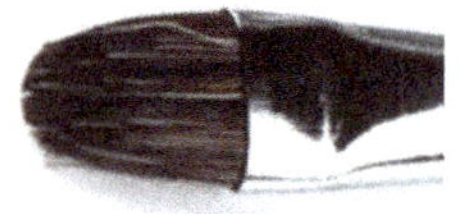

Badger - Badger brushes are typically thick at the tip and thinner at the root, giving it a bushy appearance, allowing them to hold more paint. These brushes are traditionally used for blending oil paint on canvas.

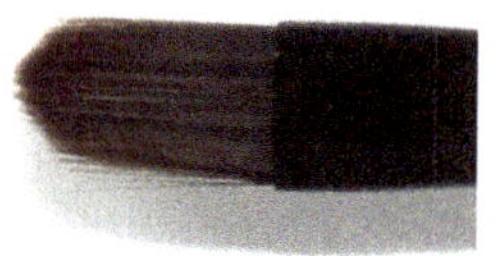

Synthetic - There are many types of synthetic brushes designed to mimic natural hairs. The major characteristic of synthetic brushes s that they reduce the appearance of brush strokes and typically last longer than natural hair brushes.

Forms of Paintbrushes

Aside from brush fiber variety, brushes come in a variety of shapes as well. Each shape is great for a specific use.

Experiment with different brushes and find the ones you are most comfortable with.

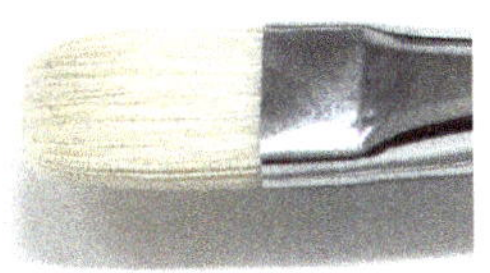

Bright - These short flat brushes are very useful for shorter strokes with more control.

Fan - Pay attention to what bristles these brushes are made of. Brushes made with natural hair are good for blending, while synthetic brushes are better for textural work.

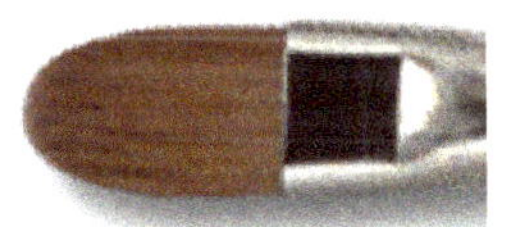

Filbert - With its unique shape, filbert brushes are great for blending, especially figures. Natural fibers are best for this type of brush as the hairs stick together when wet.

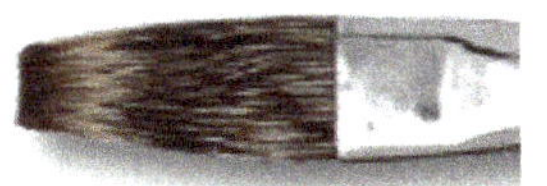

Flat - These brushes hold a lot of paint. They are great for expressive strokes and for creating fine lines.

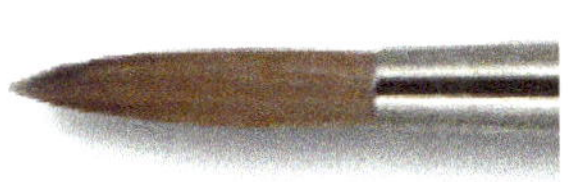

Round - Round brushes taper to a point. They are ideal for washes, large areas of color, and line work, from thick to thin. Small pointed rounds are excellent for fine detail work.

Acrylic Techniques

Mastering different techniques with acrylic paint will allow you to create a wide range of textures and add more interest in your painting. Remember to have fun and experiment.

- Layering - The first layer of a painting must be watered down so that it dries fast and so that the white canvas doesn't show through. Otherwise if it's too thick the paint will crack off. Then continue applying the second layer with less water to cover the rough canvas texture.

- Blending - Place two colors side by side and blend them together while they are still wet to create a gradual gradation from one color to the next.

- Rendering Volume - The key to using acrylic is being able to work back into it. Don't worry too much about getting details at first, work from general to detailed. If you really want details, work quickly, but don't use too much water otherwise it will show. For rendering details, it's okay to water down the paint; it may look very bright when you applied, but it will dry darker.

- Dry Brushing - Using a very small amount of paint on the brush and lightly brushing over a dry area to create a soft texture over your painting.

- Washes - Thinning down your acrylic paint with water and painting over a dry area. This creates a thin wash of paint where your underpainting can be seen through.

- Volume - Acrylics can be combined with modeling pastes of gel mediums to create a very thick surface.

- Fixing - There are a few different ways to fix problems. One way is to apply another layer once the intitial layer is dry. Another is to remove it using a remover on a soft fabric to get it off even after it is completely dry.

- Preserving - Applying a matte or gloss varnish will seal the painting. A matte varnish will finish a painting with less shine while a gloss varnish enhances glazing quality with high shine.

Arrange paints in a rainbow along the edge of the palette.

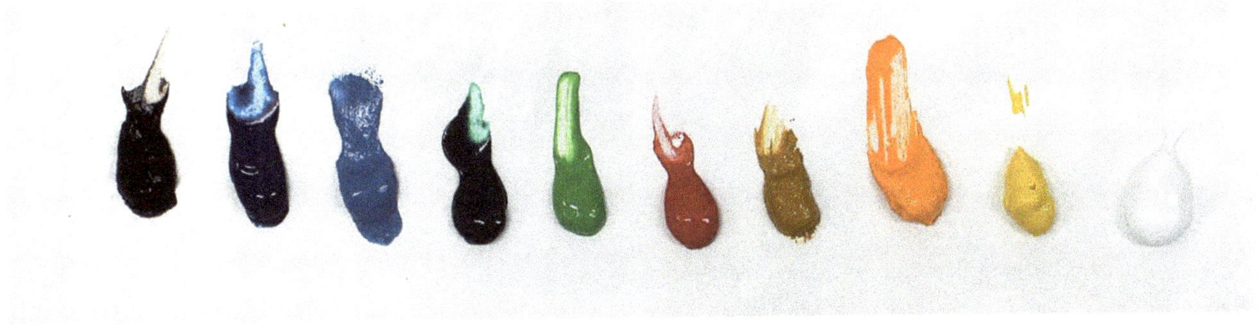

To get a better understanding of colors, try laying out the colors in the color wheel below. Use some of the colors to mix with others and see what results you get.

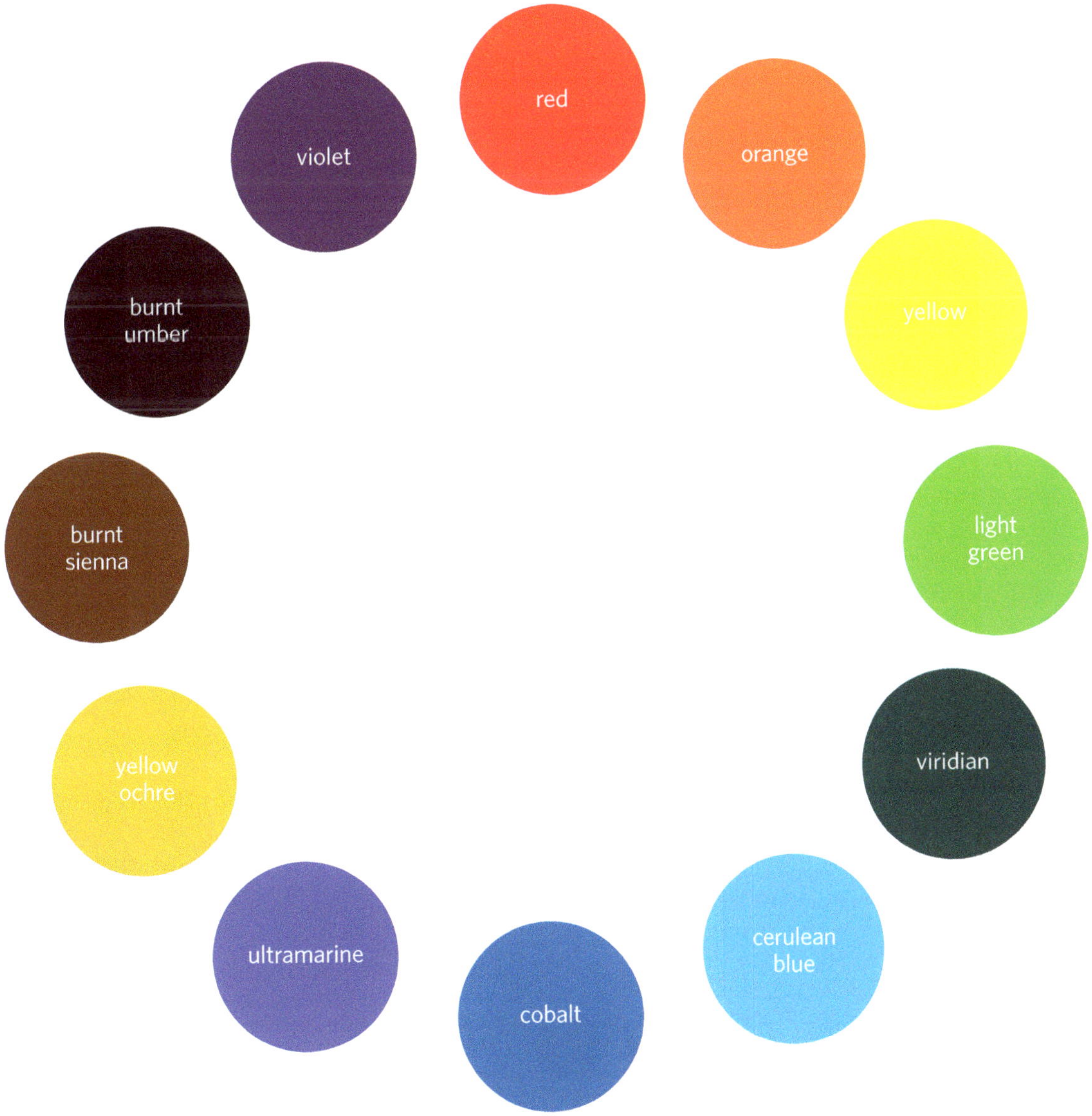

red

orange

yellow

light green

viridian

cerulean blue

cobalt

ultramarine

yellow ochre

burnt sienna

burnt umber

violet

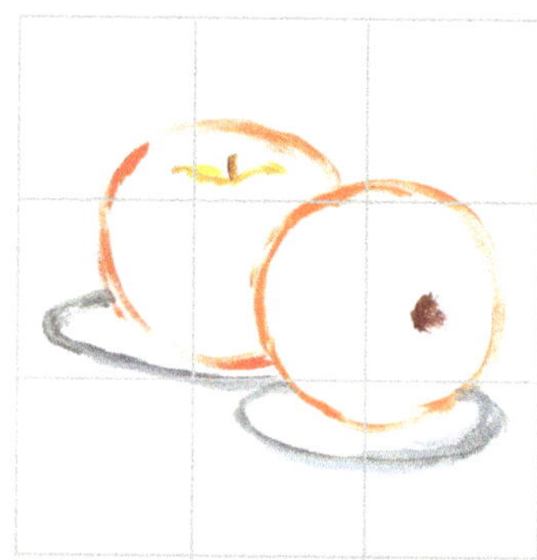

Using watered down cadmium red, outline the general shape of the apples and where their stems are. Use a light gray to outline the placement of the shadows.

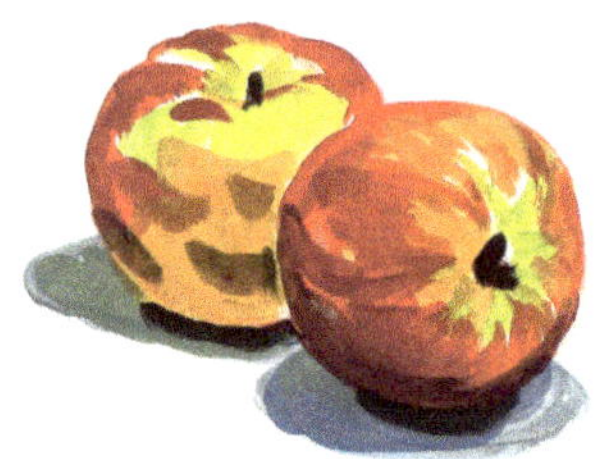

Quickly identify the areas of dark and light by roughly filling in shape of the apples with slightly watered down orange, yellow, camium red, and muted grays and blues for the shadows. Use strokes that follow the shape of the apples.

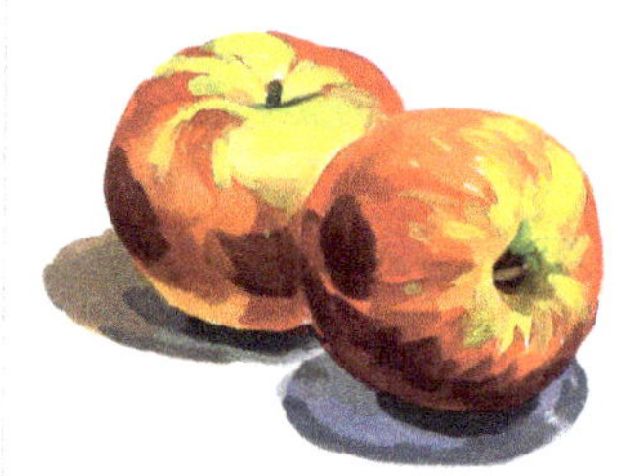

Continue to add on a wider range of colors to create a smooth surface and render the volume of the apples. Add more variations of toned down grays for the shadows by mixing colors with their compliments.

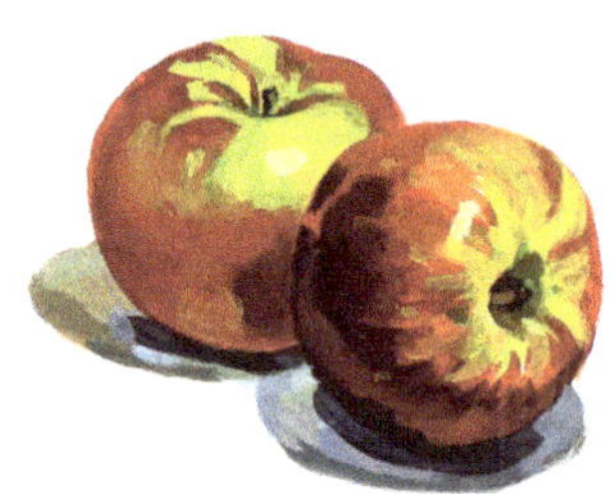

Try to create the textures of the apples by following the form with your brushstrokes. Mix in a little bit of green, black, and blues to add more range of colors and dimension. Lastly, mix white with a little bit of yellow for highlights.

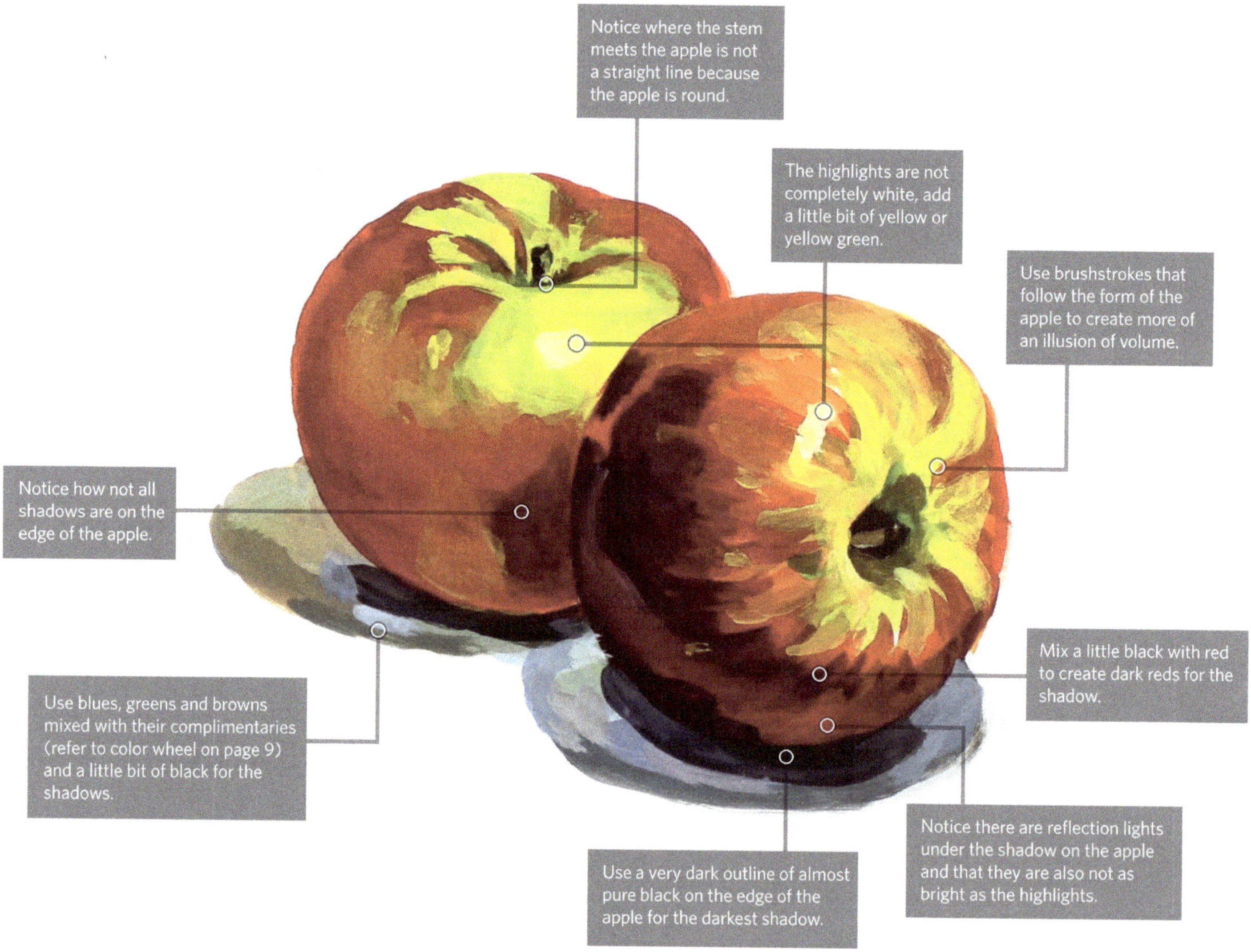

Notice where the stem meets the apple is not a straight line because the apple is round.

The highlights are not completely white, add a little bit of yellow or yellow green.

Use brushstrokes that follow the form of the apple to create more of an illusion of volume.

Notice how not all shadows are on the edge of the apple.

Mix a little black with red to create dark reds for the shadow.

Use blues, greens and browns mixed with their complimentaries (refer to color wheel on page 9) and a little bit of black for the shadows.

Notice there are reflection lights under the shadow on the apple and that they are also not as bright as the highlights.

Use a very dark outline of almost pure black on the edge of the apple for the darkest shadow.

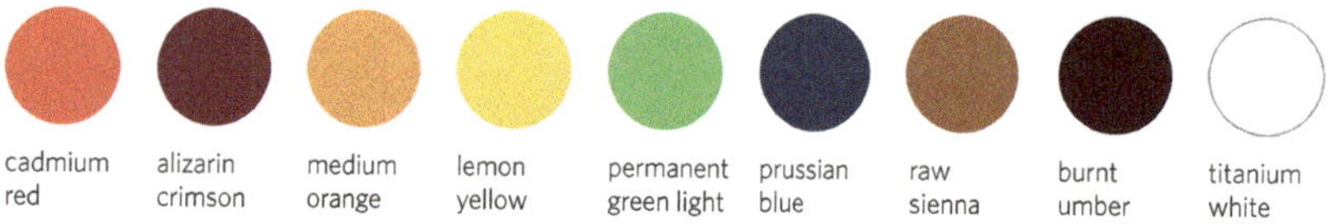

cadmium red | alizarin crimson | medium orange | lemon yellow | permanent green light | prussian blue | raw sienna | burnt umber | titanium white

Now try painting the apple yourself.

Now that you have practiced how to paint apples following a step-by-step tutorial, use the page on the right to try and paint from life. You can paint from the picture below or set up your own still life and try different variations of still life compositions.

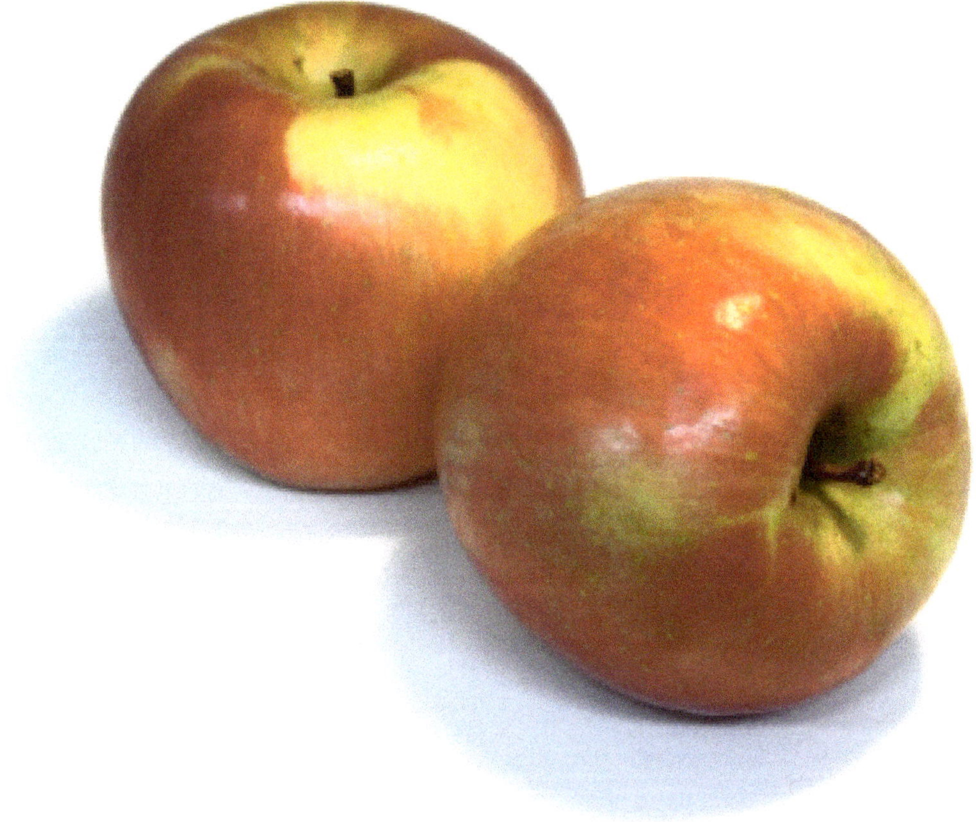

Now try painting the apple yourself without the grid.

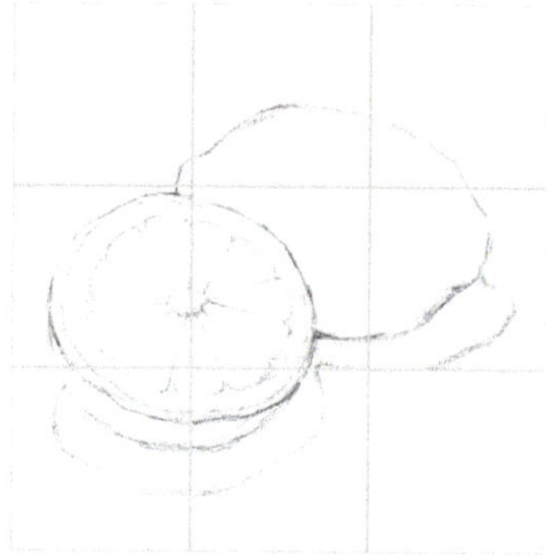

Use a pencil or watered down yellow acrlyic paint to create a general outline of the composition.

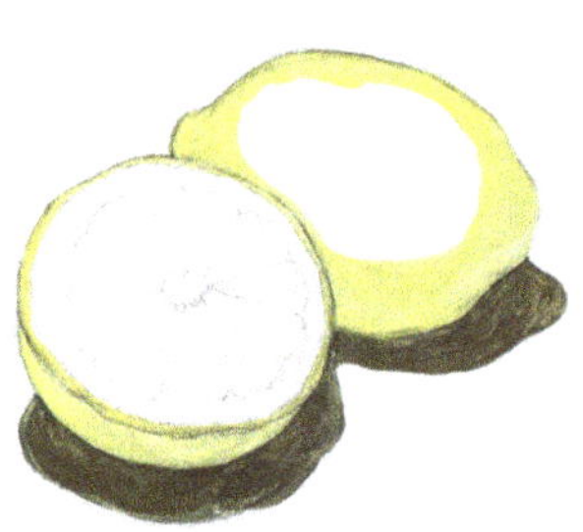

Begin identifying the general areas of shadow using lemon yellow and medium yellow mixed with burnt umber for the shadows.

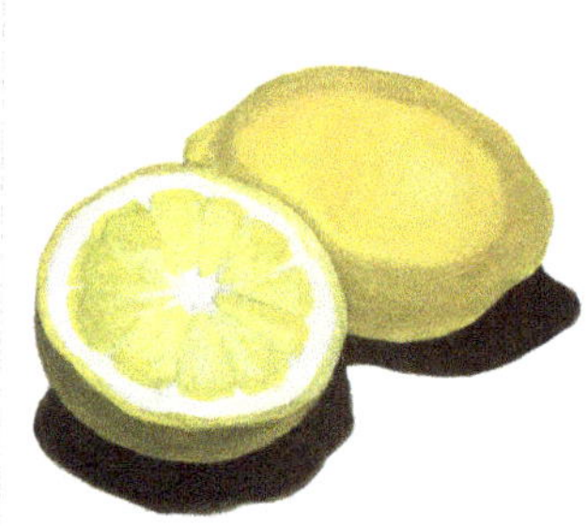

Incorporating medium yellow, lemon yellow, a little bit of permanent green light, and burnt umber, continue to block in general areas of light and dark.

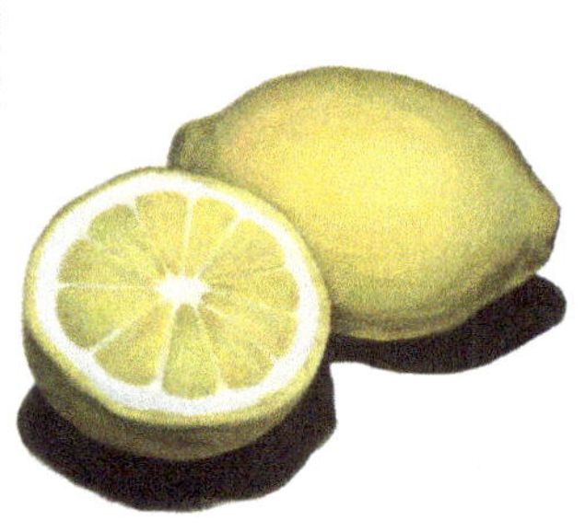

Leave rendering details, such as the texture of the lemon skin and lemon half for the very end. Focus on getting all the different tones and rendering volume by adding warm and cool colors to yellow.

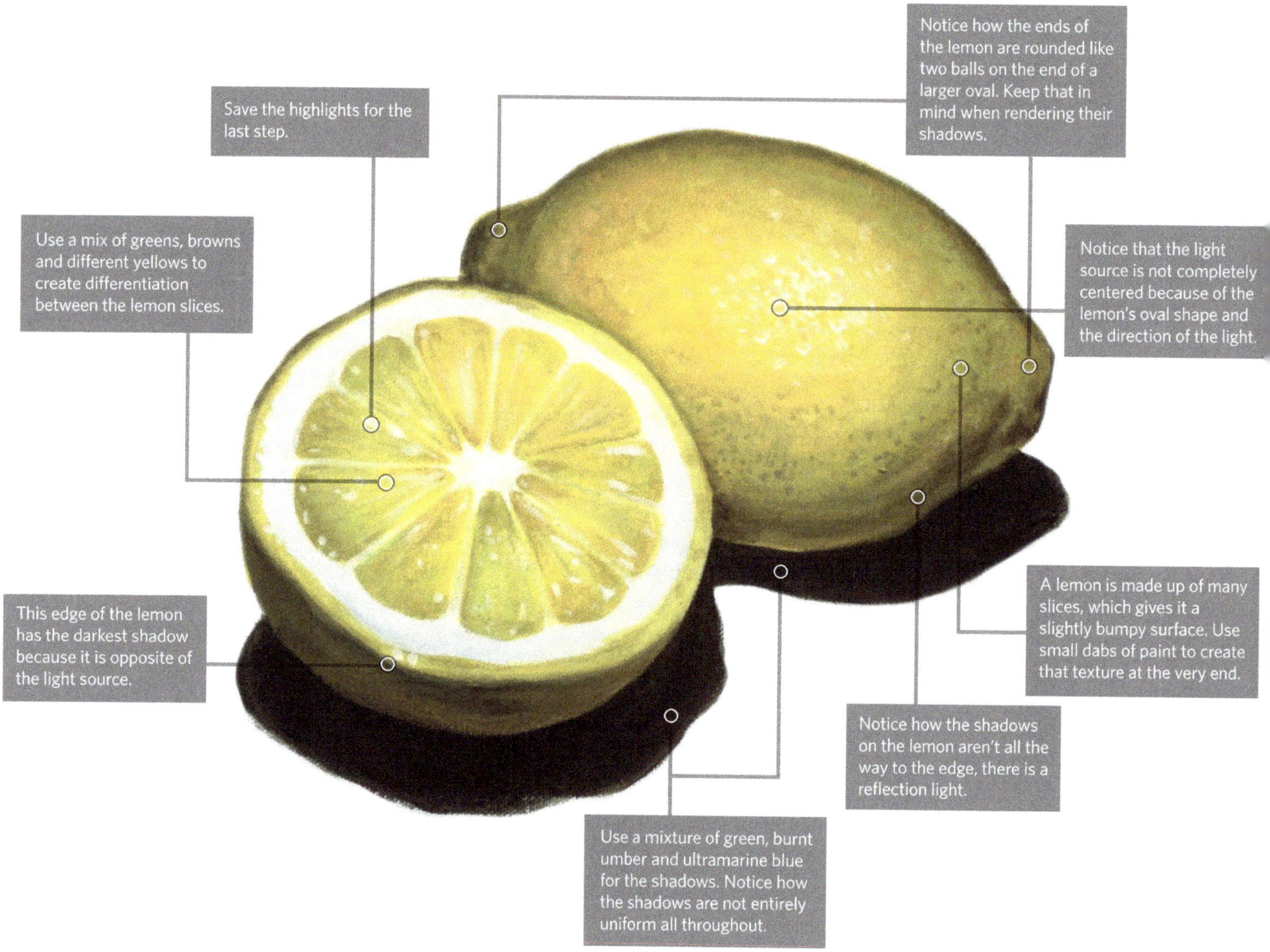

Notice how the ends of the lemon are rounded like two balls on the end of a larger oval. Keep that in mind when rendering their shadows.

Save the highlights for the last step.

Use a mix of greens, browns and different yellows to create differentiation between the lemon slices.

Notice that the light source is not completely centered because of the lemon's oval shape and the direction of the light.

A lemon is made up of many slices, which gives it a slightly bumpy surface. Use small dabs of paint to create that texture at the very end.

This edge of the lemon has the darkest shadow because it is opposite of the light source.

Notice how the shadows on the lemon aren't all the way to the edge, there is a reflection light.

Use a mixture of green, burnt umber and ultramarine blue for the shadows. Notice how the shadows are not entirely uniform all throughout.

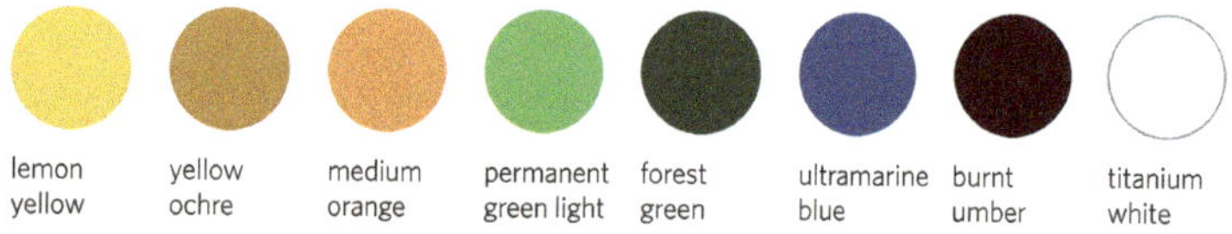

lemon yellow | yellow ochre | medium orange | permanent green light | forest green | ultramarine blue | burnt umber | titanium white

Now try painting the lemon yourself.

Now that you have practiced how to paint lemons following a step-by-step tutorial, use the page on the right to try and paint from life. You can paint from the picture below or set up your own still life and try different variations of still life compositions.

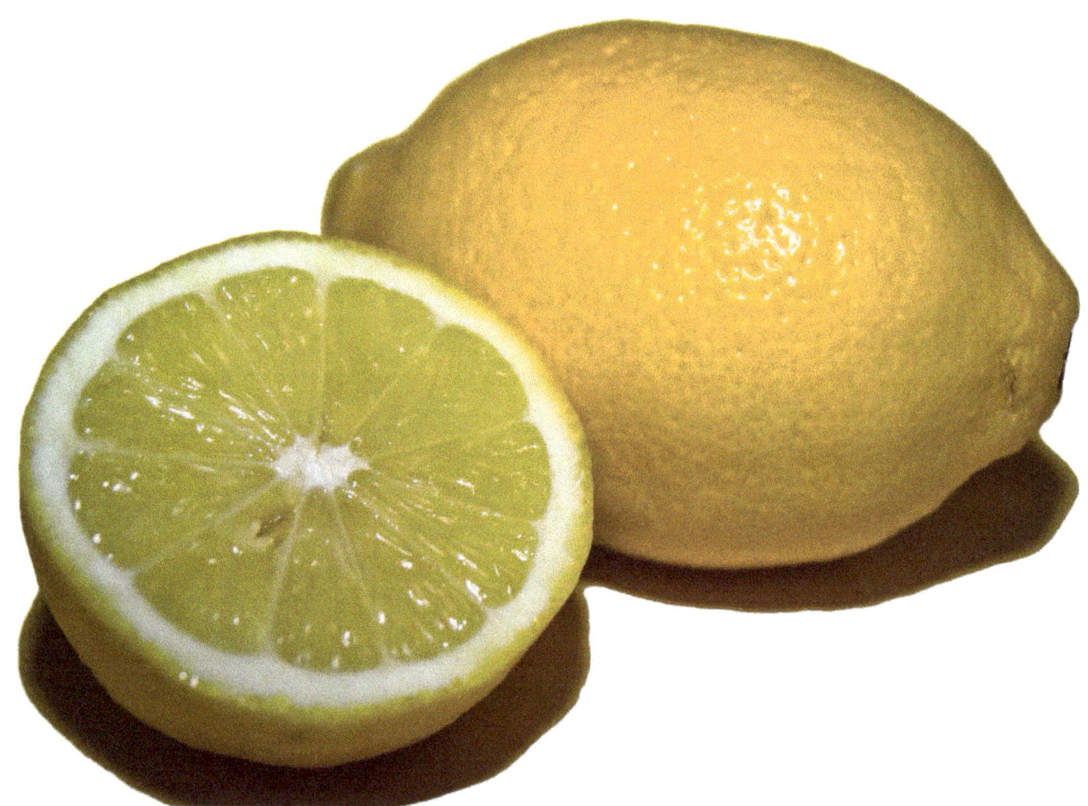

Now try painting the lemon yourself without the grid.

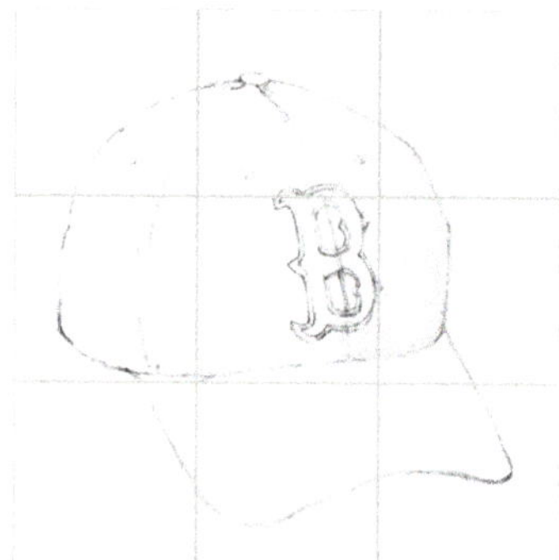
Keep these lines parallel to one another.

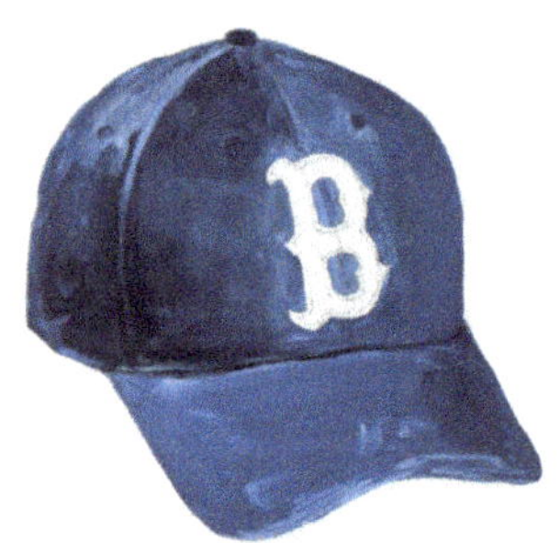
Block in all of the middle tones first using a middle tone blue to establish a baseline color. Then begin adding the highlights and darker tones.

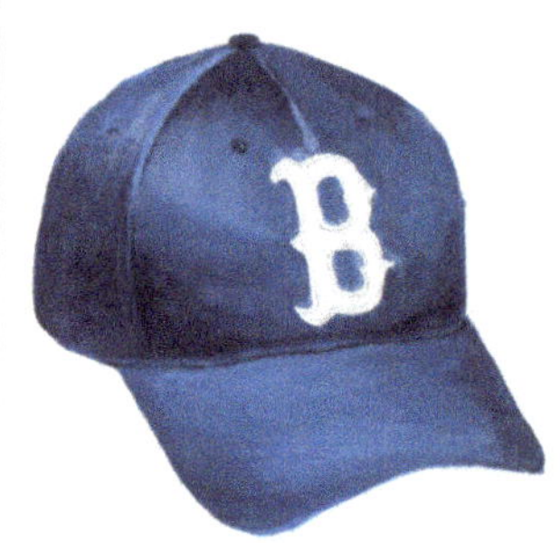
Blend more with the brushes to create a smoother texture. At the same time, create a more curved volume.

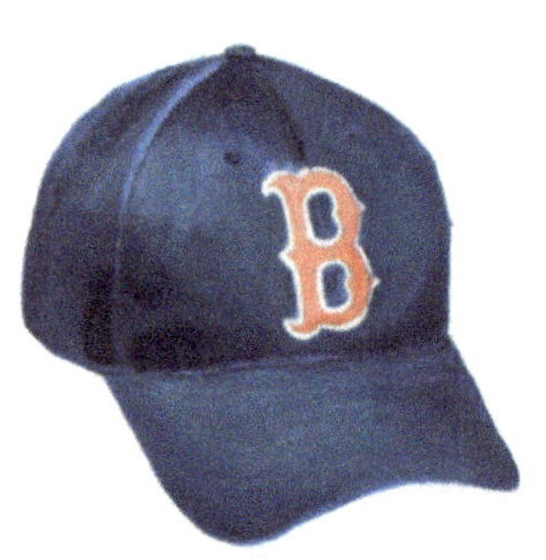
To create the shadows on the object, mix the middle tone color with the complimentary color, in this case use blue and orange. Save the details for the last step, such as the stitches, holes, and the button on top.

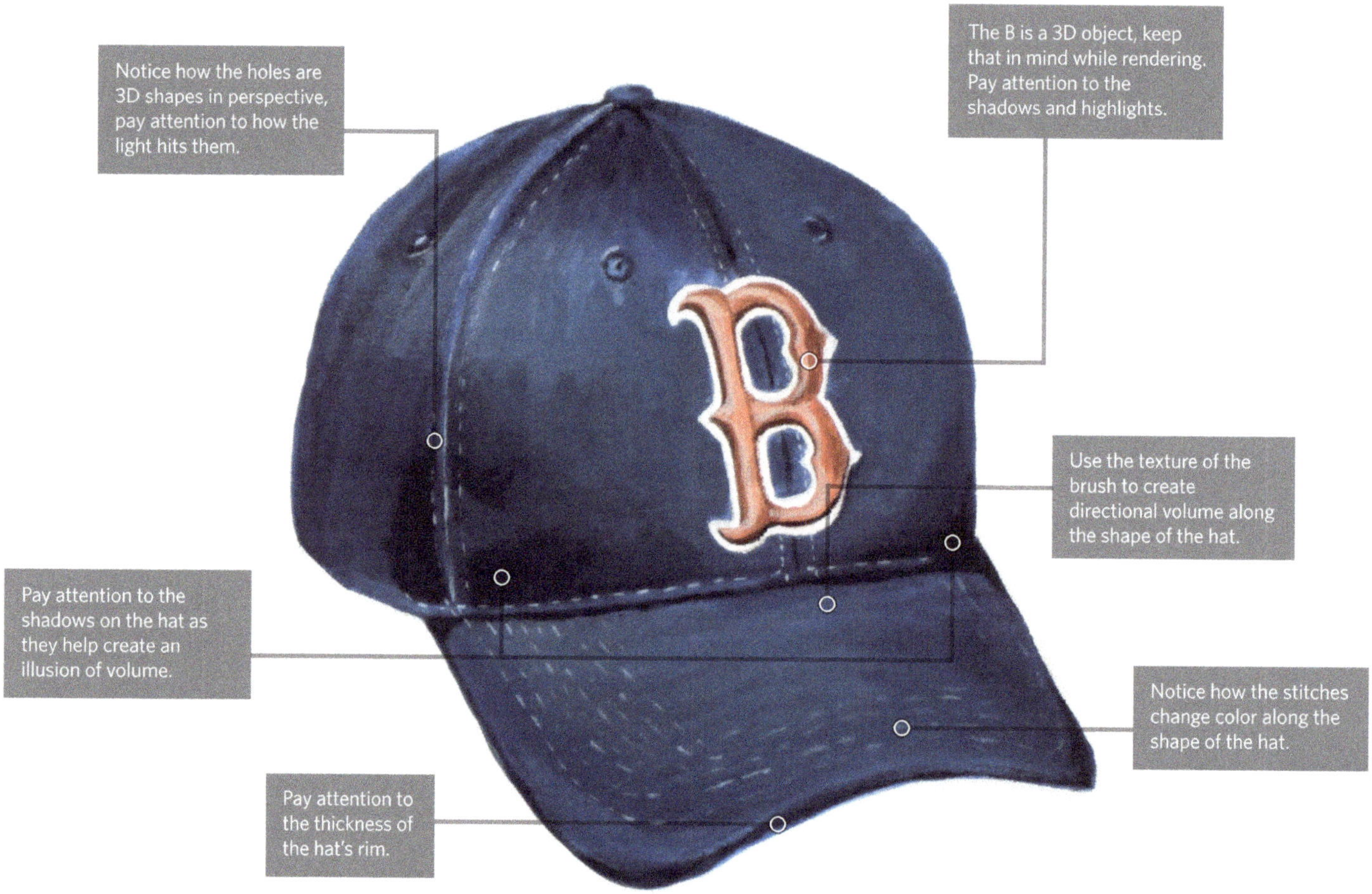

Notice how the holes are 3D shapes in perspective, pay attention to how the light hits them.

The B is a 3D object, keep that in mind while rendering. Pay attention to the shadows and highlights.

Use the texture of the brush to create directional volume along the shape of the hat.

Pay attention to the shadows on the hat as they help create an illusion of volume.

Notice how the stitches change color along the shape of the hat.

Pay attention to the thickness of the hat's rim.

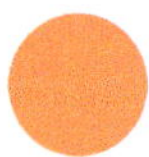
cadmium orange

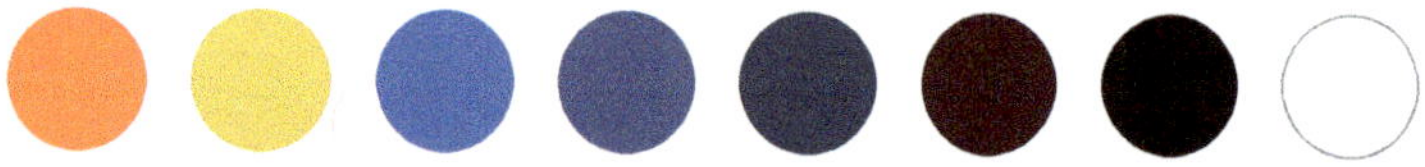

lemon yellow

cobalt blue

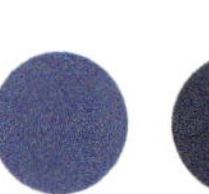
ultramarine blue

prussian blue

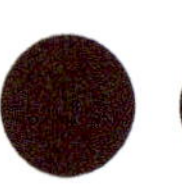
burnt umber

mars black

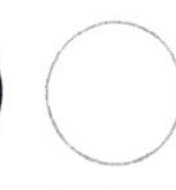
titanium white

Now try painting the hat yourself.

Now that you have practiced how to paint a baseball hat following a step-by-step tutorial, use the page on the right to try and paint from life. You can paint from the picture below or set up your own still life and try different variations of still life compositions.

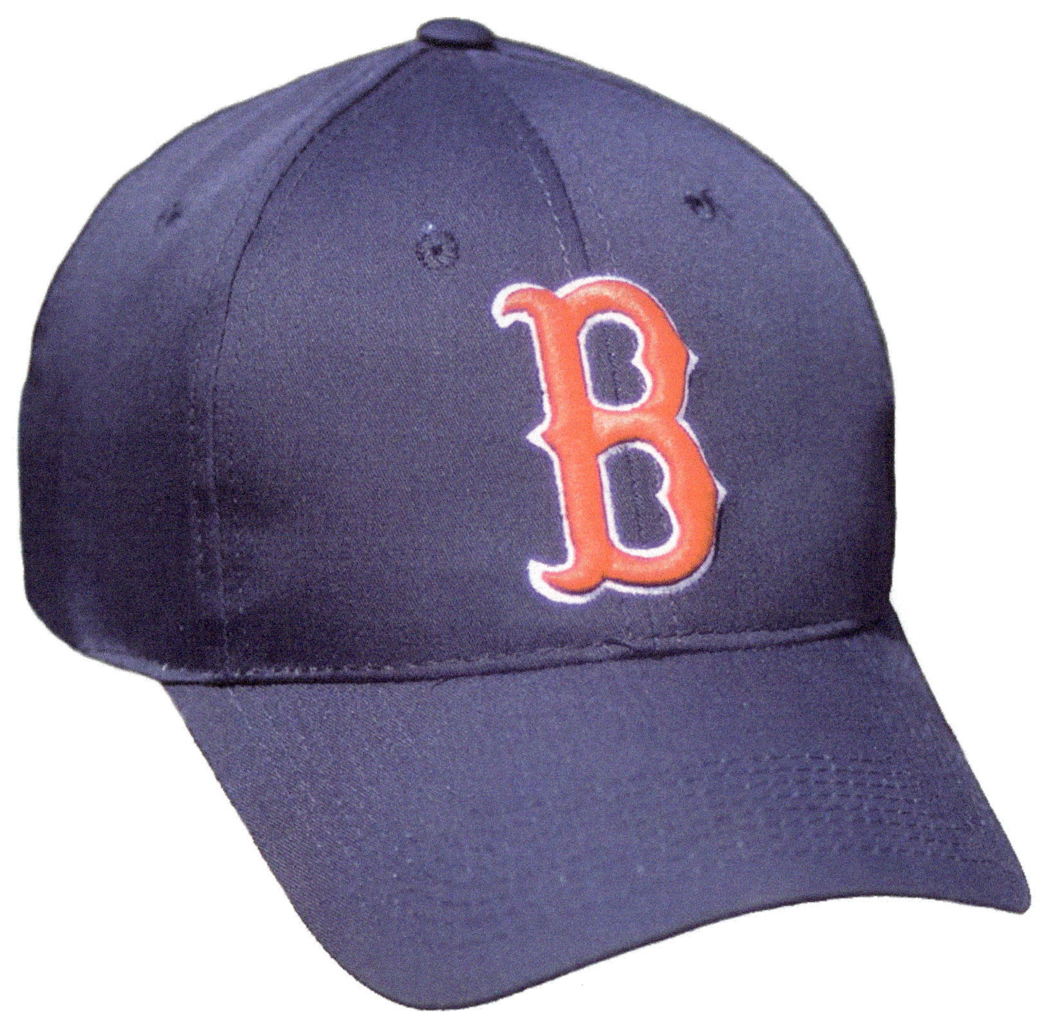

Now try painting the baseball hat yourself without the grid.

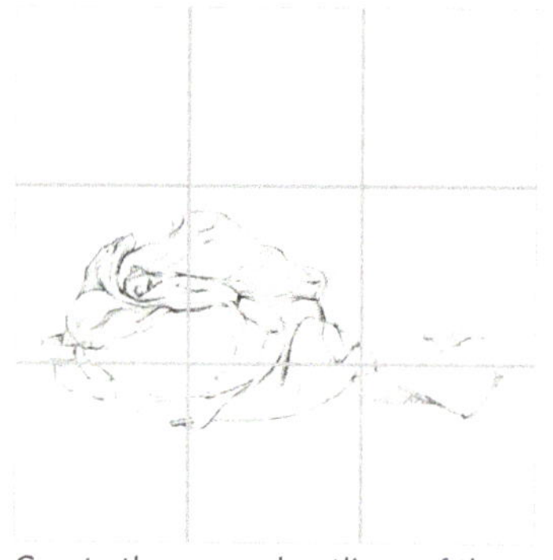

Create the general outlines of the shapes and folds of the garment in pencil.

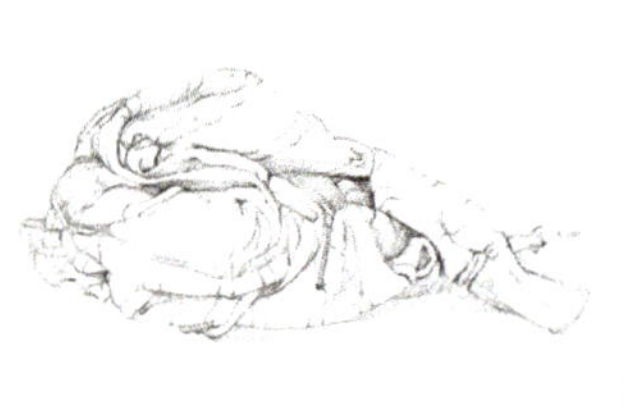

Identify general areas of shadow in pencil and create a more detailed rendering.

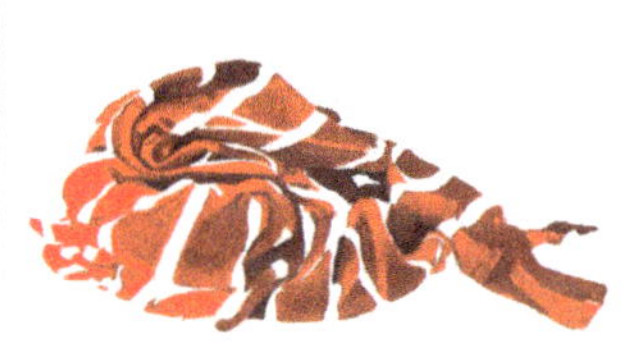

Begin blocking in areas of color using cadmium red for light areas and mixing it with a little bit of black for areas of shadow.

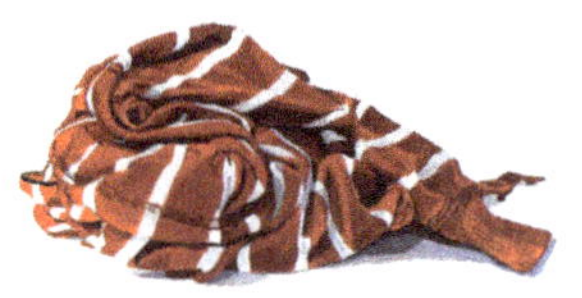

Continue to render shadow and light using cool tones mixed into your reds. Mix a cool gray for the shadow on the table.

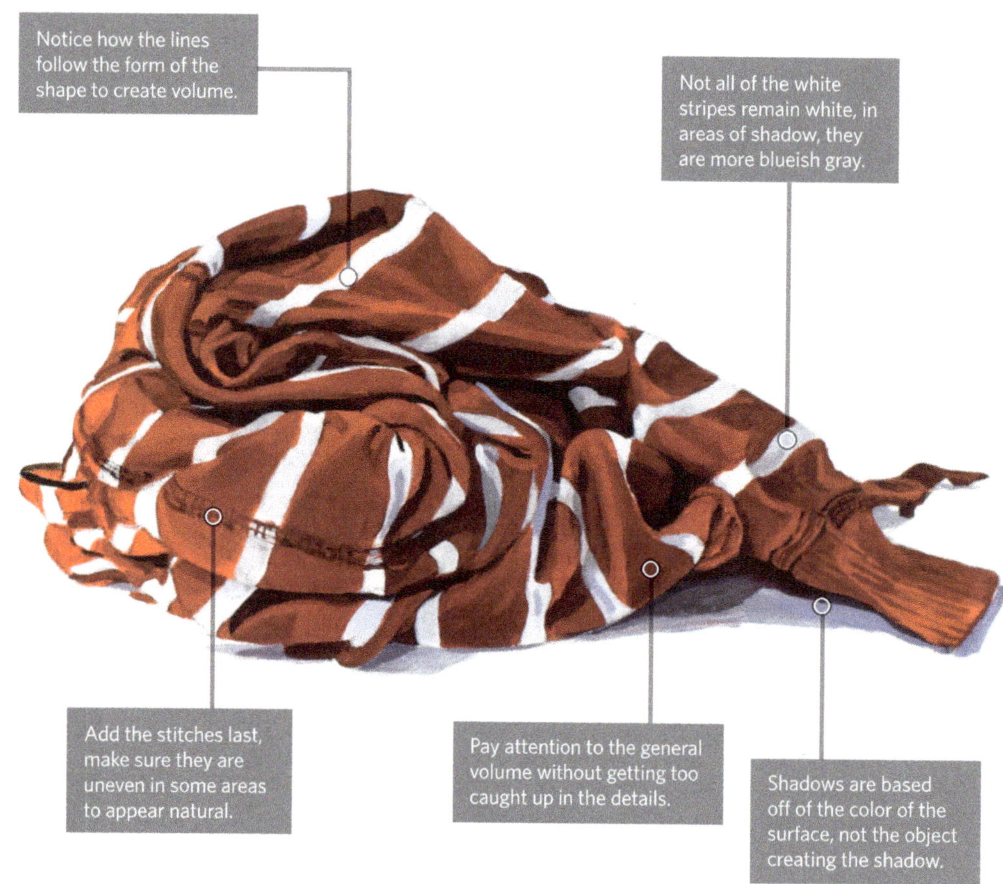

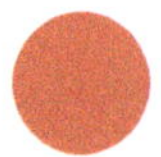
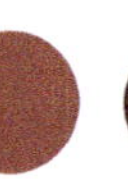

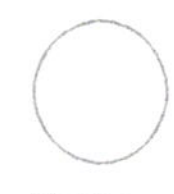

cadmium red

cadmium red deep

burnt umber

prussian blue

mars black

titanium white

Now try painting the red garment yourself.

Now that you have practiced how to paint a crumpled garment following a step-by-step tutorial, use the page on the right to try and paint from life. You can paint from the picture below or set up your own still life and try different variations of still life compositions.

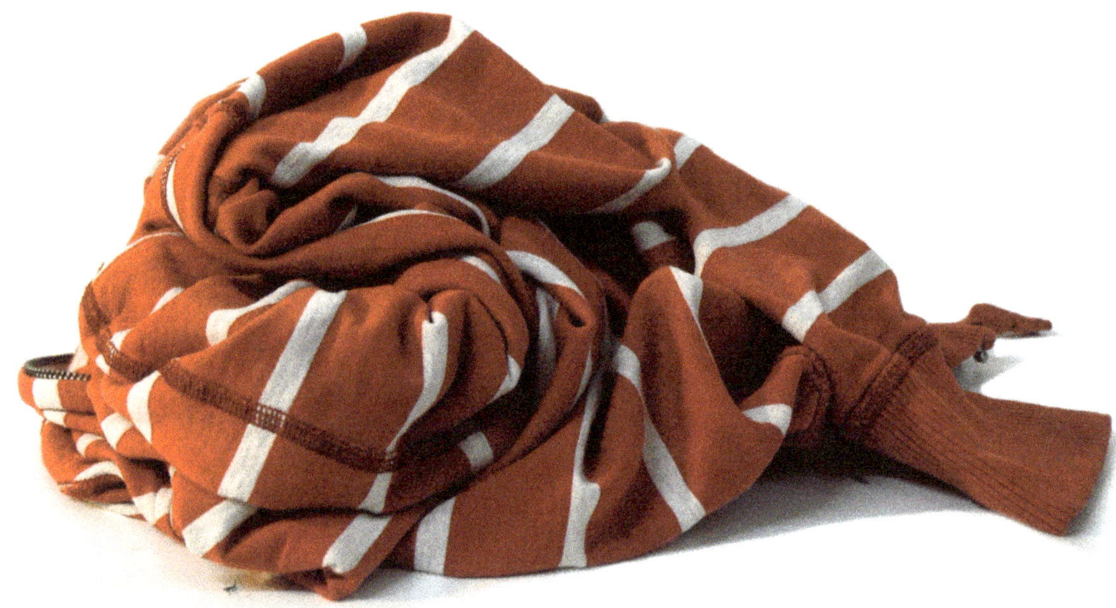

RED GARMENT: PRACTICE II

Now try painting the red garment yourself without the grid.

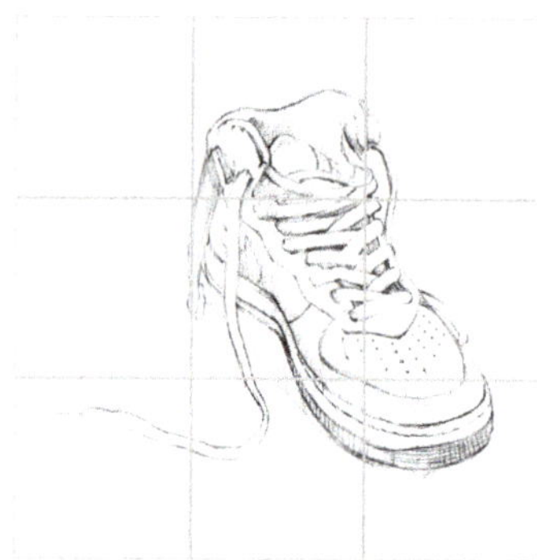

Using vine charcoal, sketch the general geometric shape of the shoe with a center line through the middle to identify the major planes of the shoe.

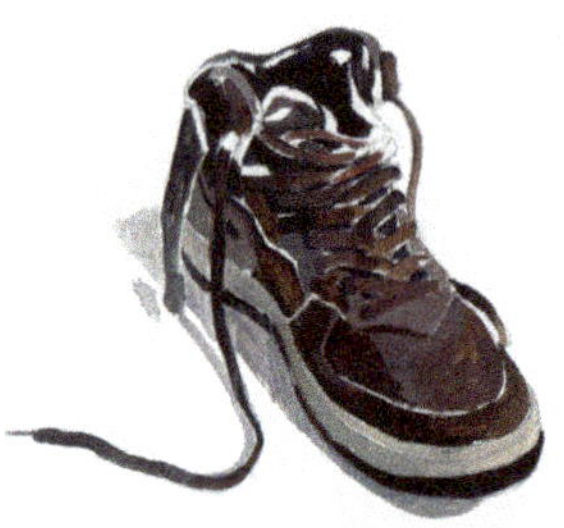

Identify general details, then identify the direction of the light source and block in the general areas of shadow using medium tone browns.

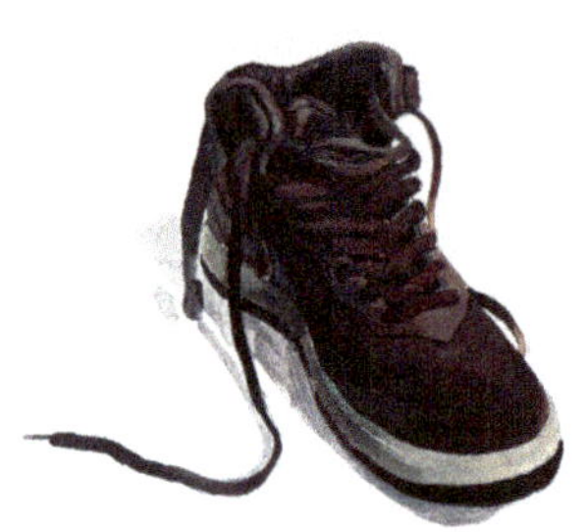

Continue to identify the darks, lights, and middle tones using a combination of dark to light browns. Mix in cool and warm colors to enhance depth and richness of your browns.

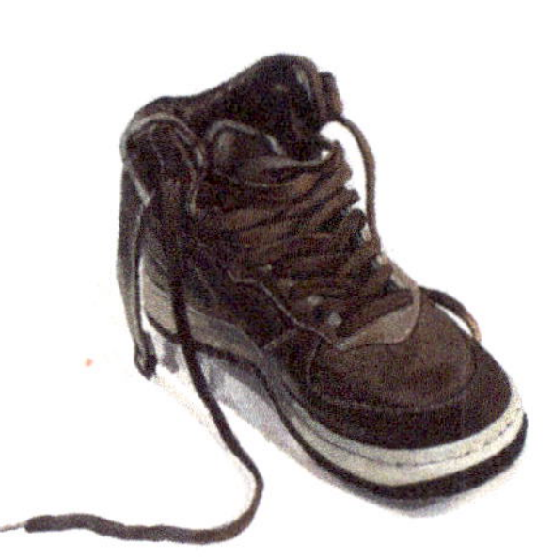

Make sure to use the entire range of tones to fully develop your painting. Only on the last step define the details in the stitching and holes of the shoe.

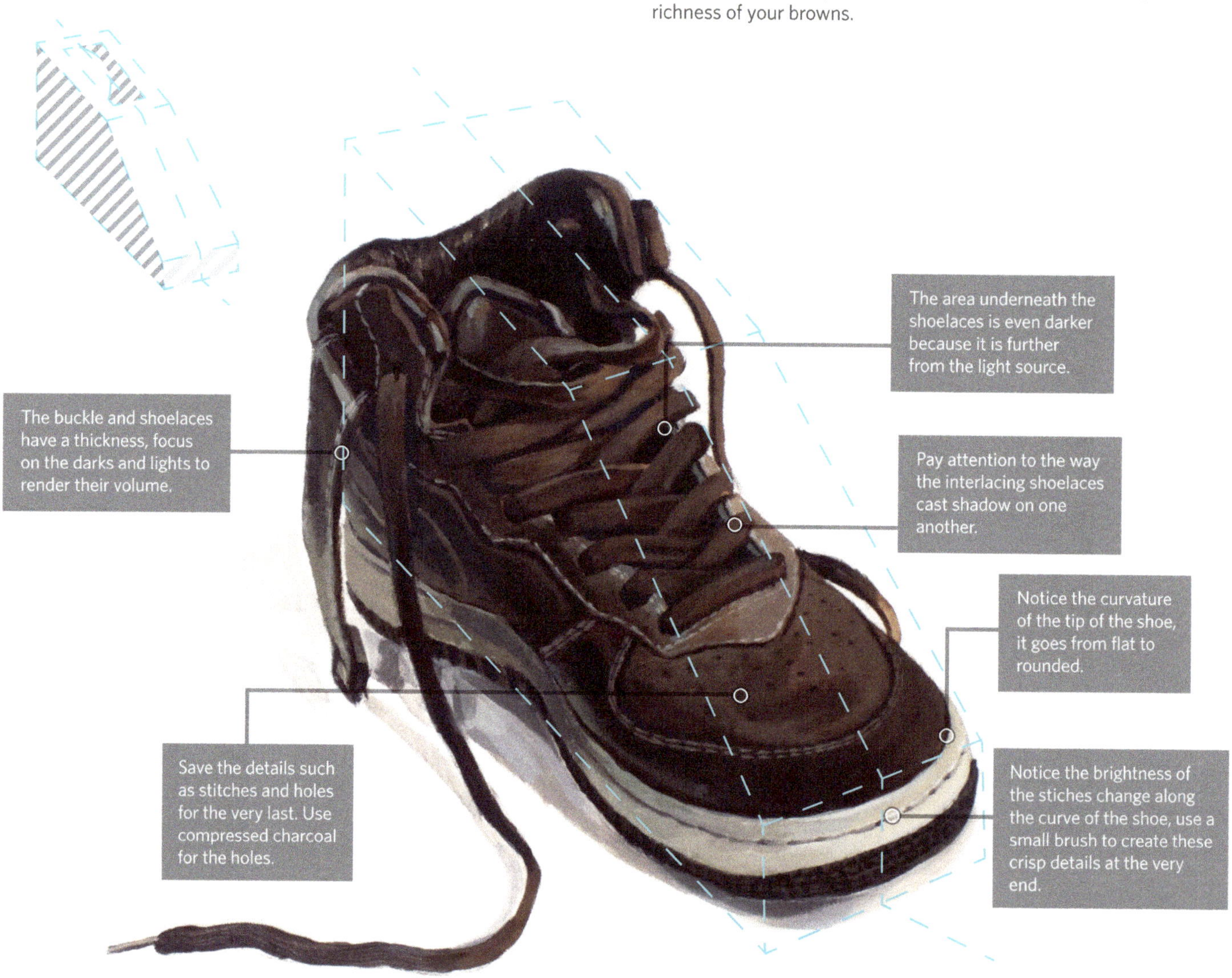

The area underneath the shoelaces is even darker because it is further from the light source.

The buckle and shoelaces have a thickness, focus on the darks and lights to render their volume.

Pay attention to the way the interlacing shoelaces cast shadow on one another.

Notice the curvature of the tip of the shoe, it goes from flat to rounded.

Save the details such as stitches and holes for the very last. Use compressed charcoal for the holes.

Notice the brightness of the stiches change along the curve of the shoe, use a small brush to create these crisp details at the very end.

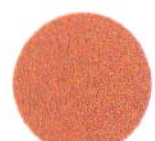

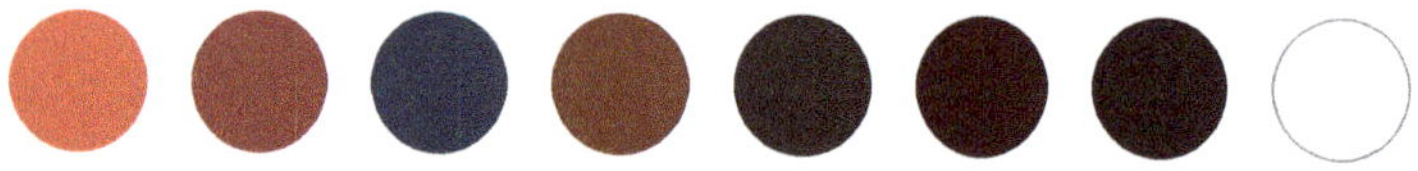

cadmium red

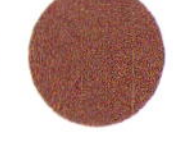

cadmium red deep

prussian blue

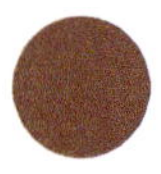

burnt sienna

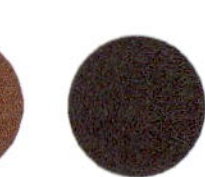

raw umber

burnt umber

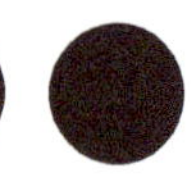

mars black

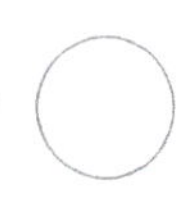

titanium white

Now try painting the shoes yourself.

Now that you have practiced how to paint shoes following a step-by-step tutorial, use the page on the right to try and paint from life. You can paint from the picture below or set up your own still life and try different variations of still life compositions.

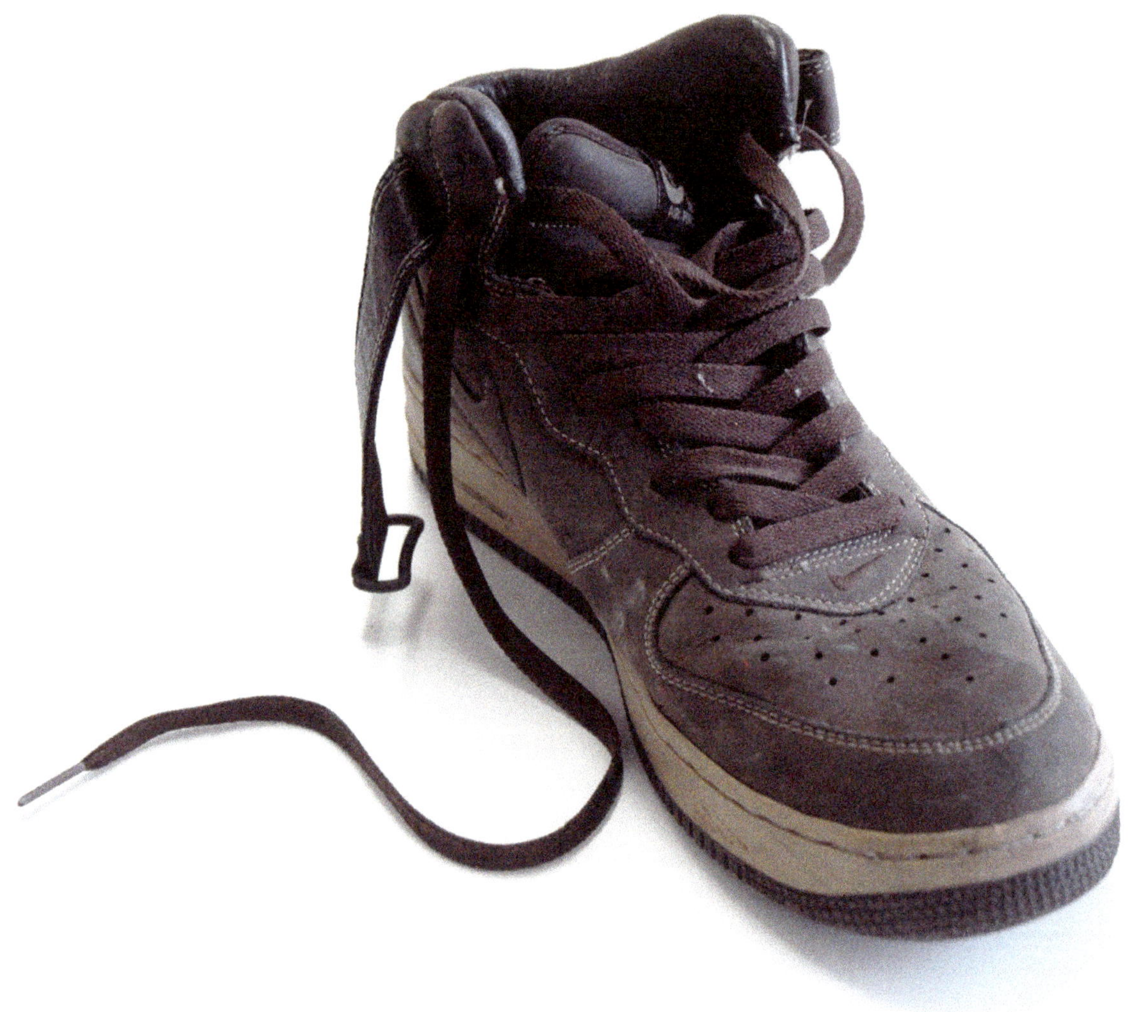

SHOE: PRACTICE II

Now try painting the shoe yourself without the grid.

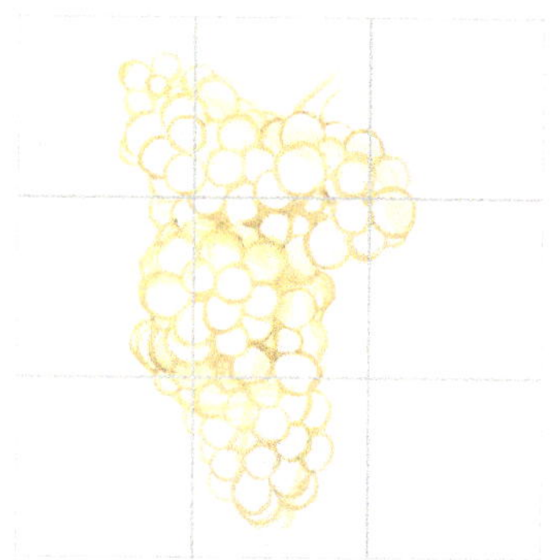

Paint the overall shape of the grapes, then add in general circles for the individual grapes in a light color like yellow.

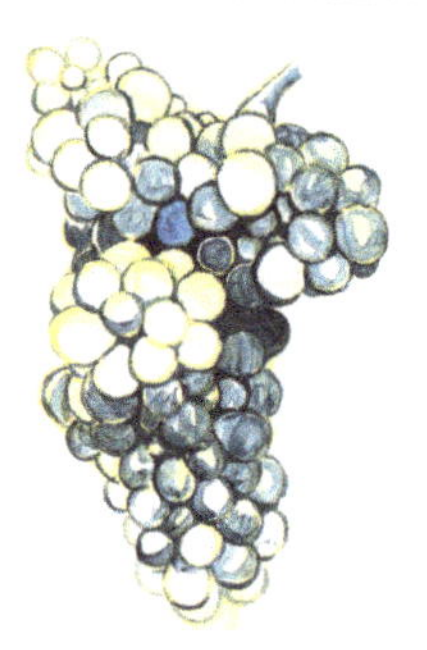

Pay attention to the overall volume but also the individual volumes of each grape. Start with cool colors to warm colors, so begin with using prussian blue.

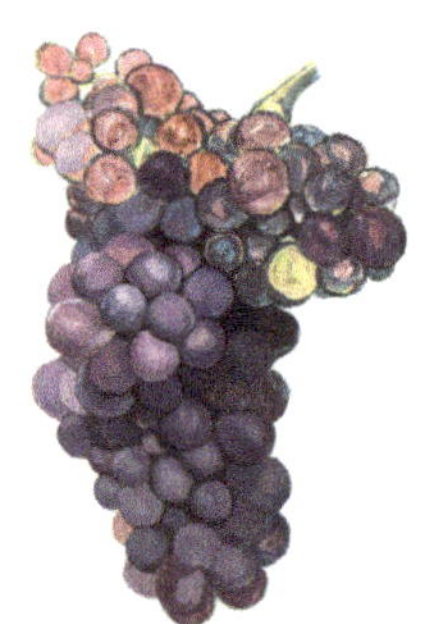

Using different warm and cool colors, make a variety of different purples. Stick with the colors of the reference photo instead of making up your own purples along the way.

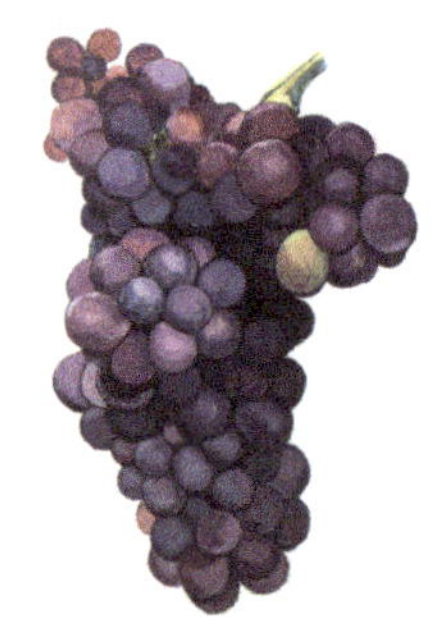

One by one, create the general colors and volume of each grape. Don't worry about the specific details just yet. Put highlights and look at the general shape of the grape for the very last step.

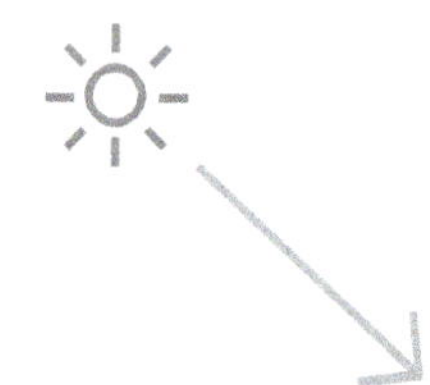

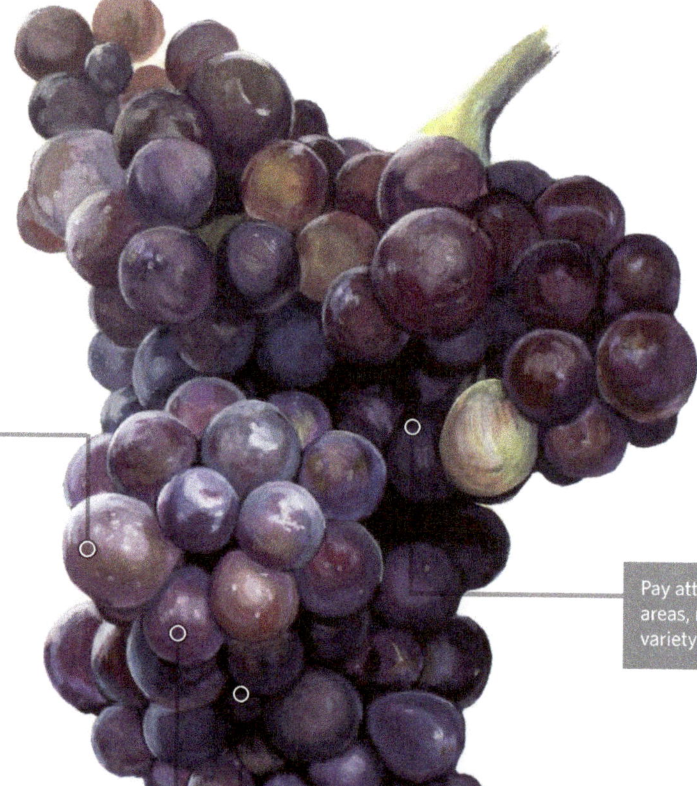

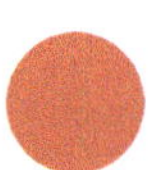
cadmium red

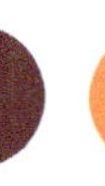
alizarin crimson

cadmium orange

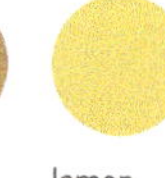
yellow ochre

lemon yellow

permanent green light

cerulean blue

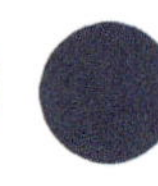
ultramarine blue

prussian blue

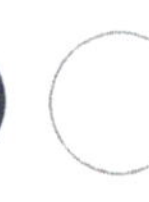
titanium white

Now try painting the grapes yourself.

Now that you have practiced how to paint grapes following a step-by-step tutorial, use the page on the right to try and paint from life. You can paint from the picture below or set up your own still life and try different variations of still life compositions.

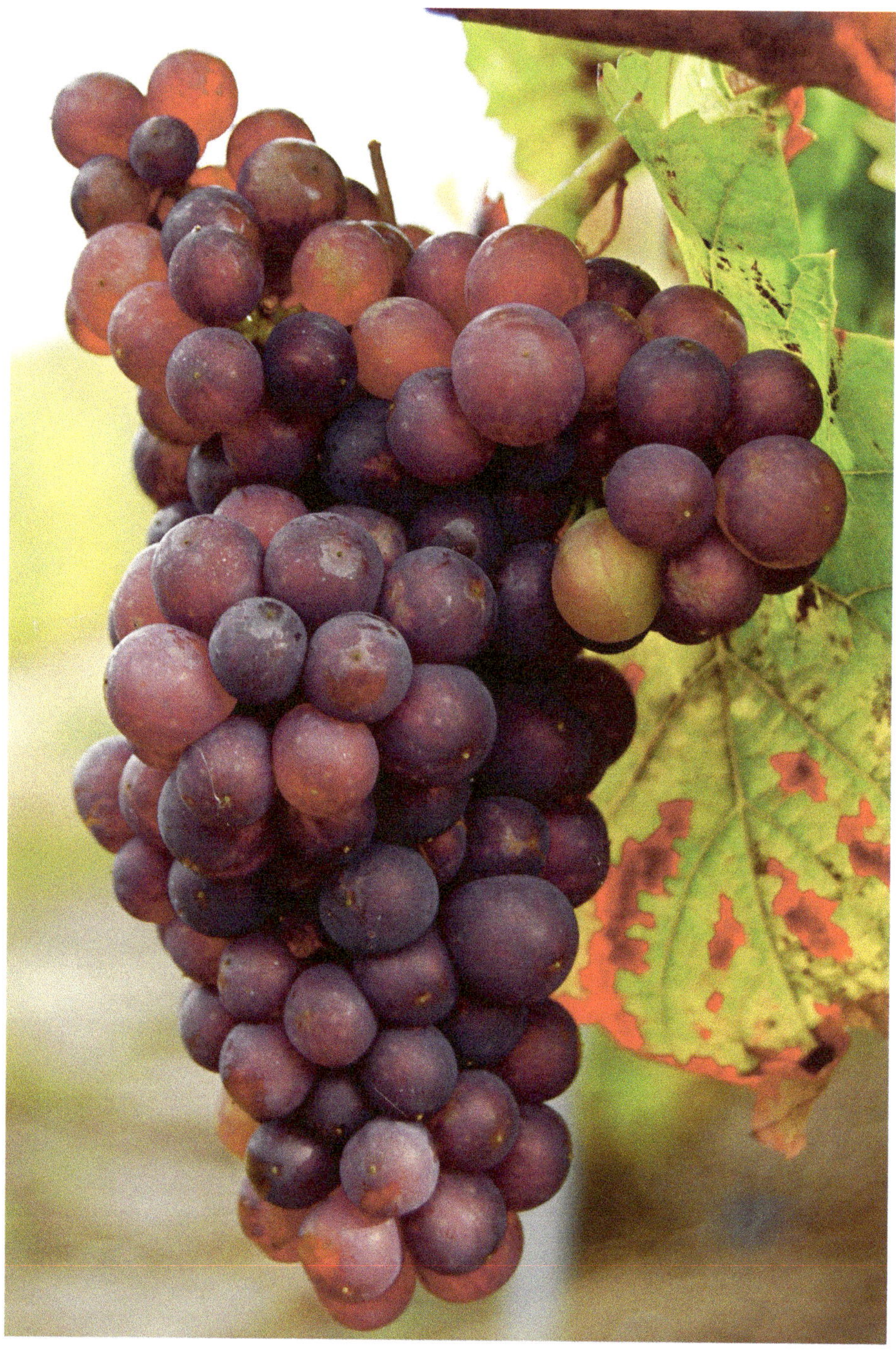

Now try painting the grapes yourself without the grid.

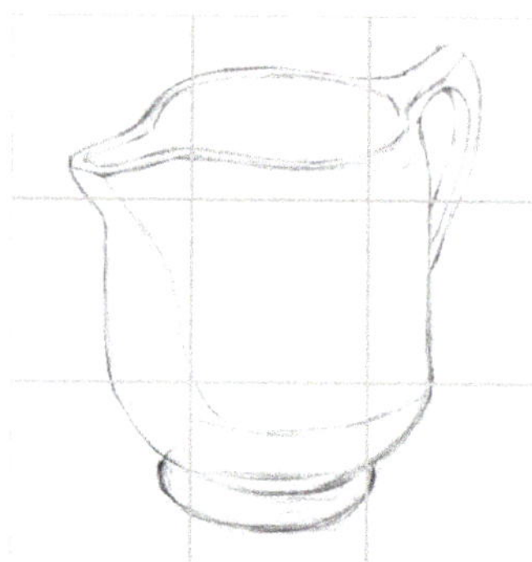

Create a general outline of the cup using pencil.

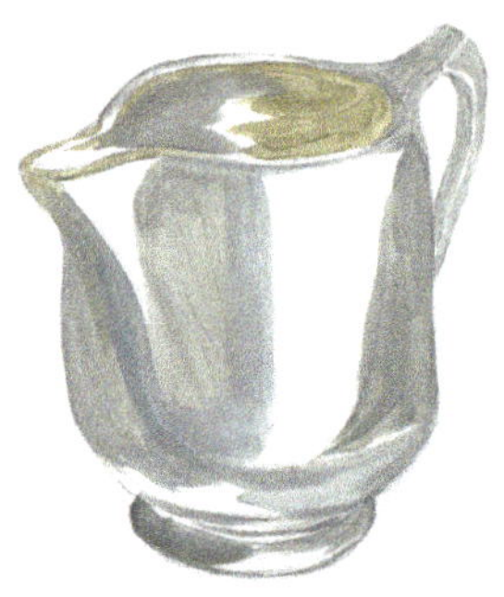

Block in the general areas of shadow and highlight using watered down washes of paint.

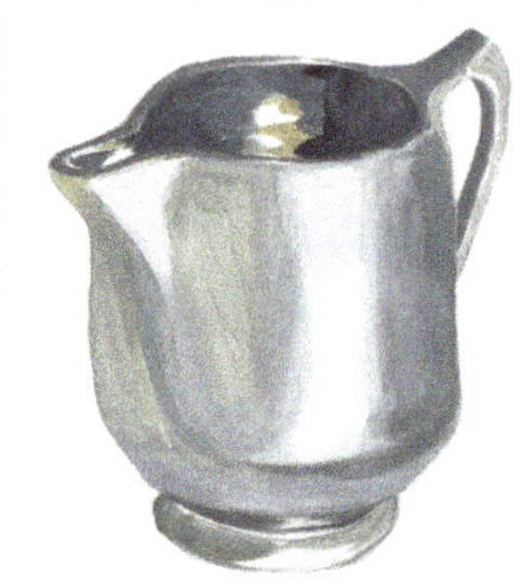

Pay attention to the volume, but also to the contrasting highlights and shadows that metal creates. There is an even balance between volume and highlights, so be very careful about defining either one.

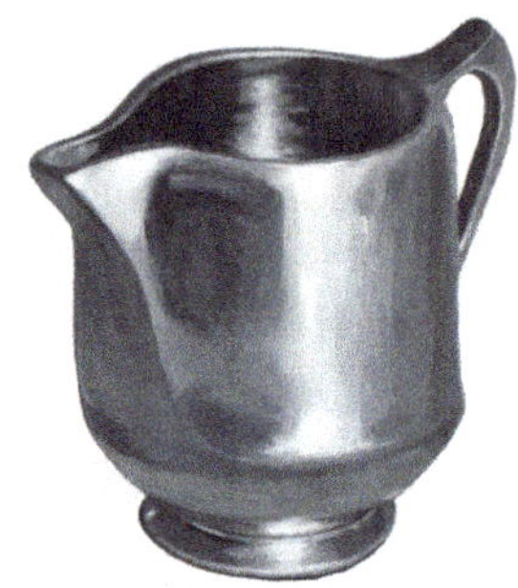

Generally use cool tones, but refrain from using pure black and white, there are little bits of blue, green, and warm colors mixed in. It's important for the highlights to be smooth gradients. Make sure that the outlines are sharp to clearly define the shape.

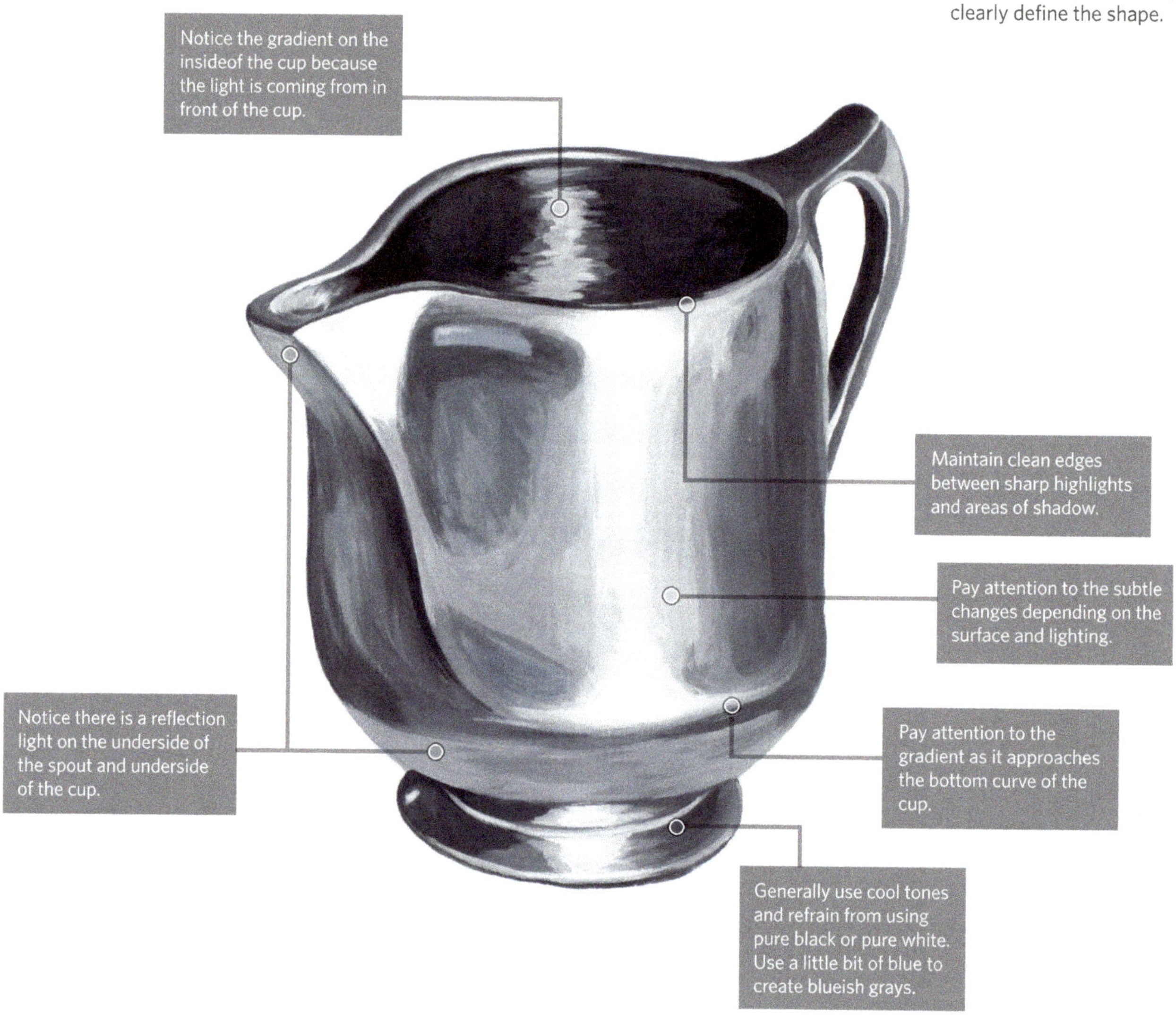

Notice the gradient on the insideof the cup because the light is coming from in front of the cup.

Maintain clean edges between sharp highlights and areas of shadow.

Pay attention to the subtle changes depending on the surface and lighting.

Notice there is a reflection light on the underside of the spout and underside of the cup.

Pay attention to the gradient as it approaches the bottom curve of the cup.

Generally use cool tones and refrain from using pure black or pure white. Use a little bit of blue to create blueish grays.

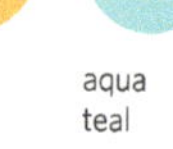
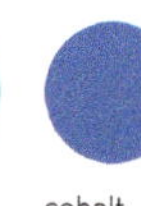

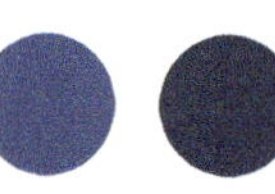
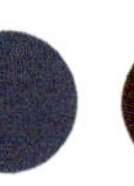
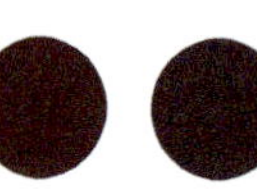
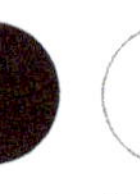
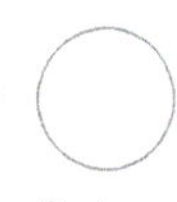

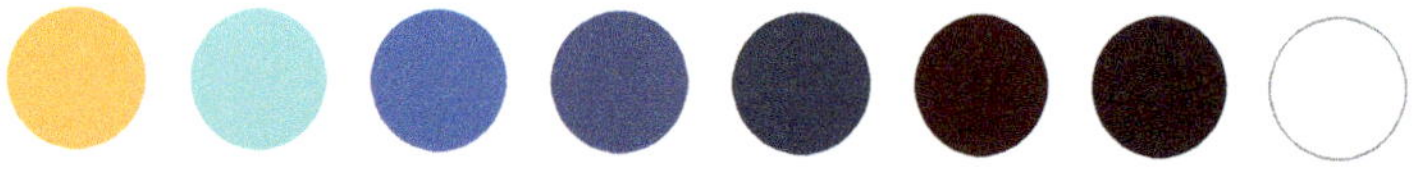

amber | aqua teal | cobalt blue | ultramarine blue | prussian blue | burnt umber | mars black | titanium white

Now try painting the metal cup yourself.

Now that you have practiced how to paint a metal cup following a step-by-step tutorial, use the page on the right to try and paint from life. You can paint from the picture below or set up your own still life and try different variations of still life compositions.

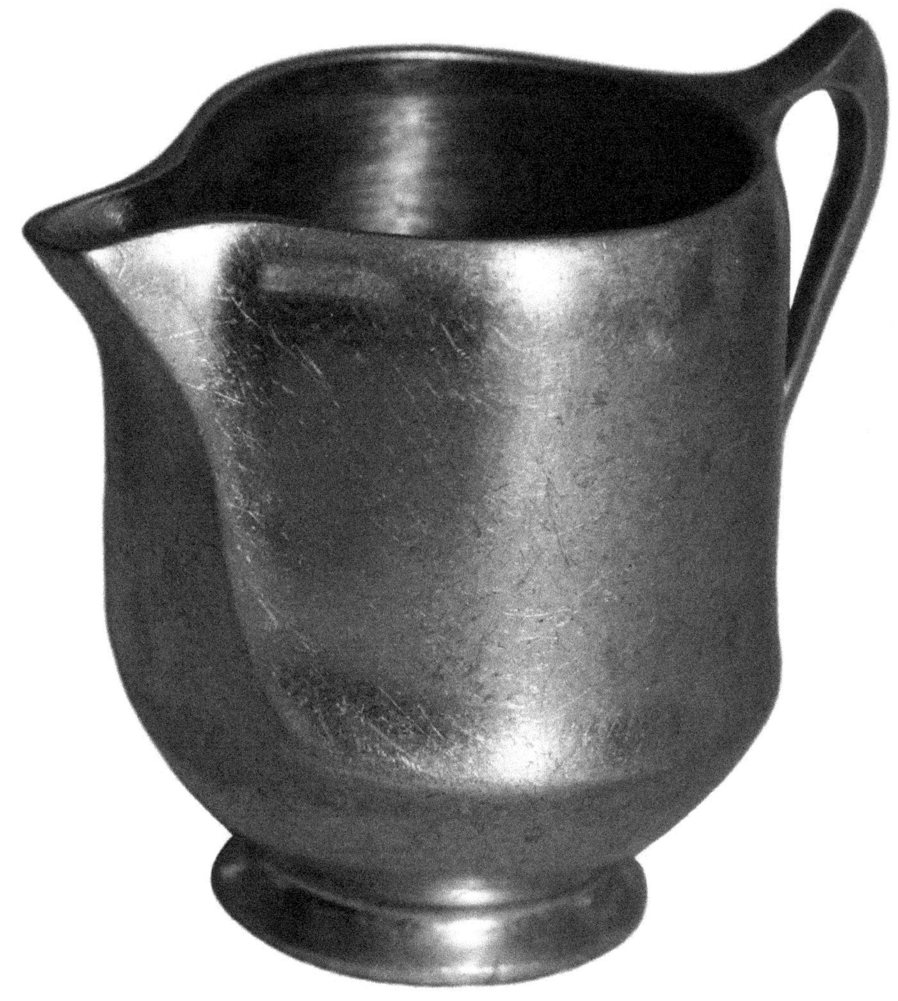

Now try painting the metal cup yourself without the grid.

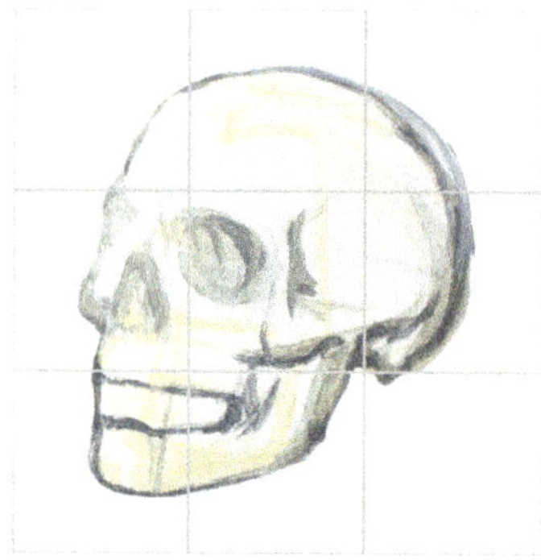

Make a rough outline or general shape of the skull using watered down burnt umber mixed with a little bit of prussian blue. Think of a real person's head.

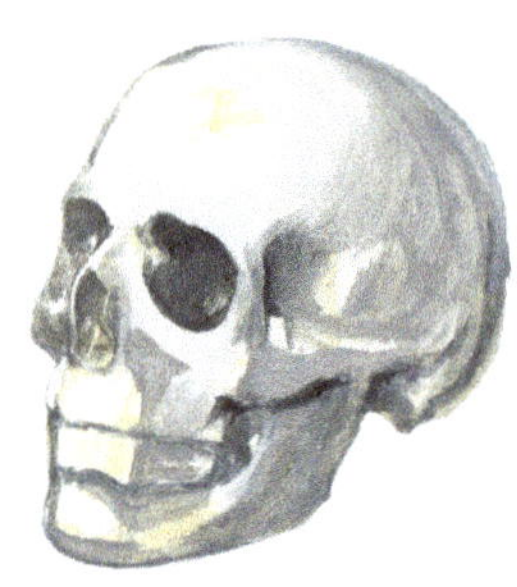

Identify the general areas of shadow and areas of light by blocking in the general direction of light.

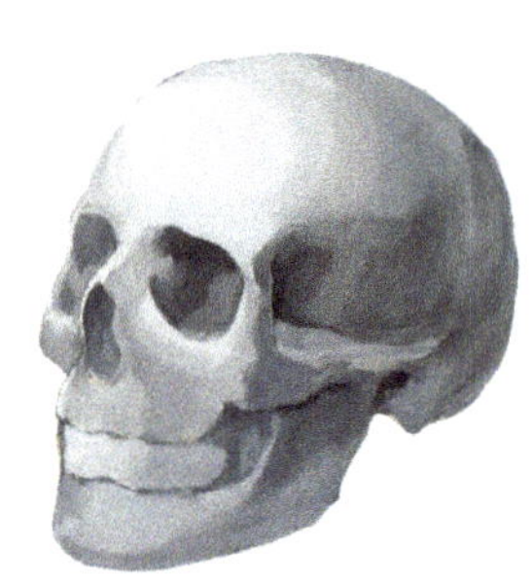

Since the lighting is a little yellow, the lighter areas are slightly yellow toned and the shadows should be cool toned. Keep a general shape of the teeth until everything looks right as a whole.

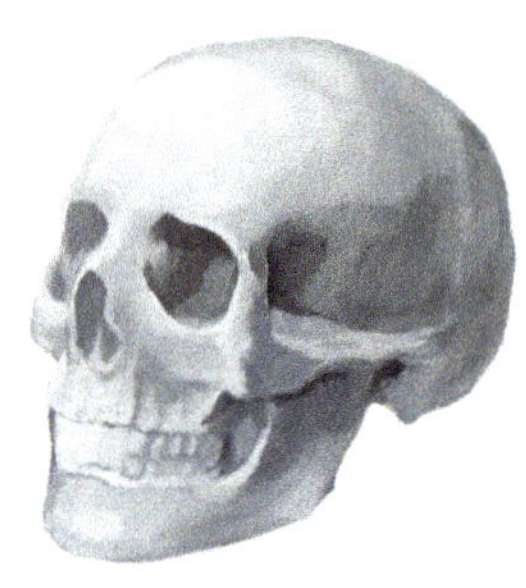

Define the structure of the bones and bone lines. Create volume from top to bottom and left to right. Also pay attention to the areas of depth in the skull using deep shadows. Dont draw lines for the teeth, paint shadows from the shadow side to the light side.

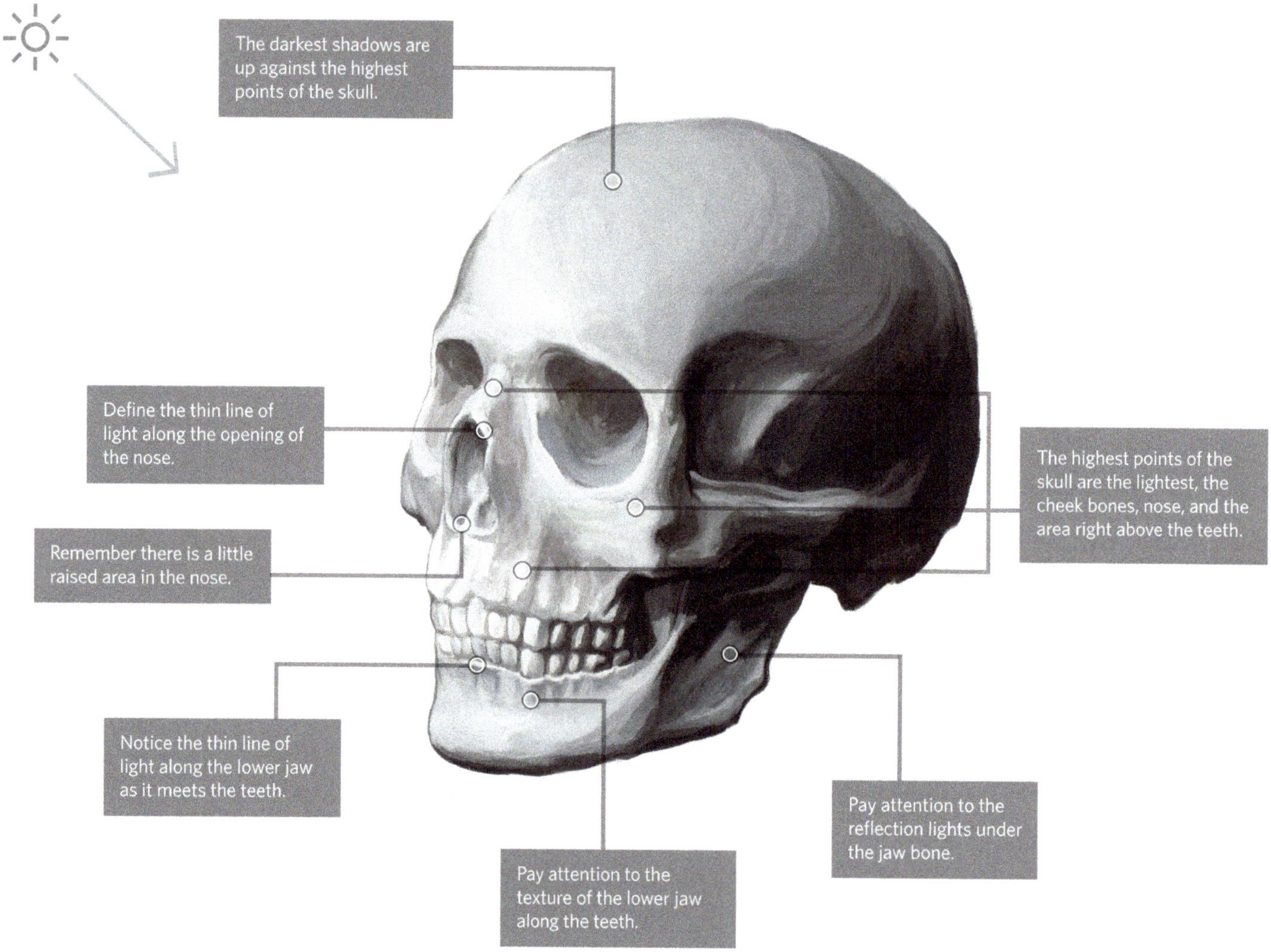

The darkest shadows are up against the highest points of the skull.

Define the thin line of light along the opening of the nose.

Remember there is a little raised area in the nose.

The highest points of the skull are the lightest, the cheek bones, nose, and the area right above the teeth.

Notice the thin line of light along the lower jaw as it meets the teeth.

Pay attention to the reflection lights under the jaw bone.

Pay attention to the texture of the lower jaw along the teeth.

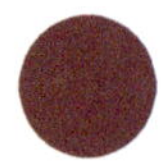
alizarin crimson

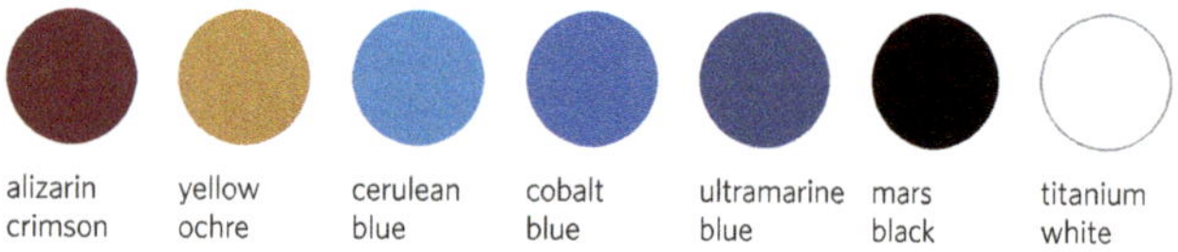

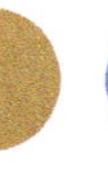
yellow ochre

cerulean blue

cobalt blue

ultramarine blue

mars black

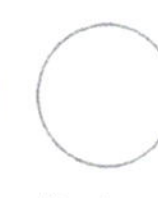
titanium white

Now try painting the skull yourself.

Now that you have practiced how to paint a skull following a step-by-step tutorial, use the page on the right to try and paint from life. You can paint from the picture below or set up your own still life and try different variations of still life compositions.

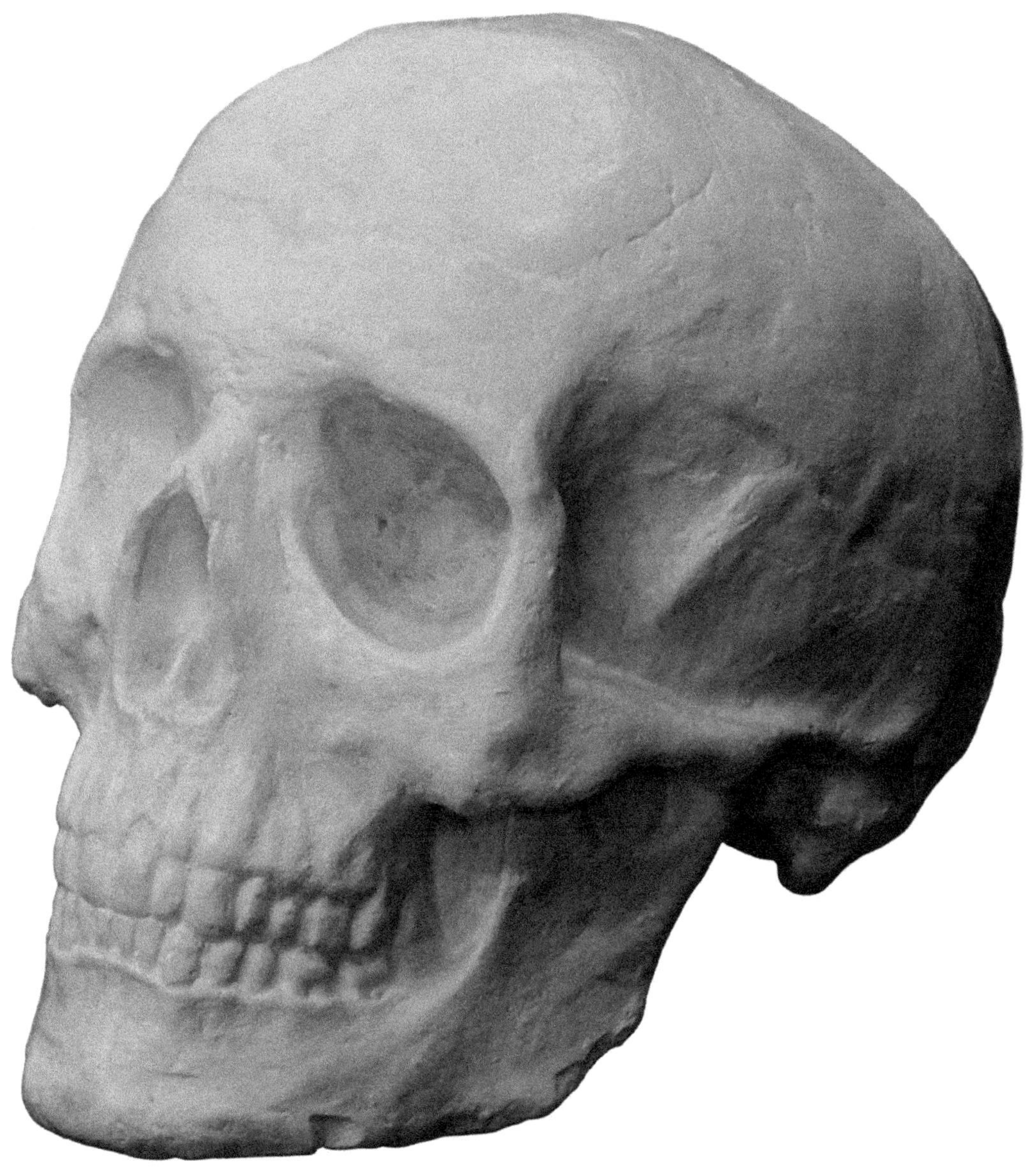

SKULL: PRACTICE II

Now try painting the skull yourself without the grid.

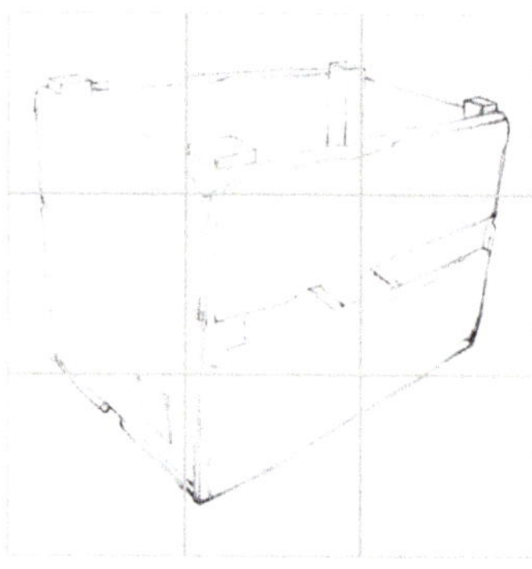

Perspective is very important for the sketch. Use lines to guide you.

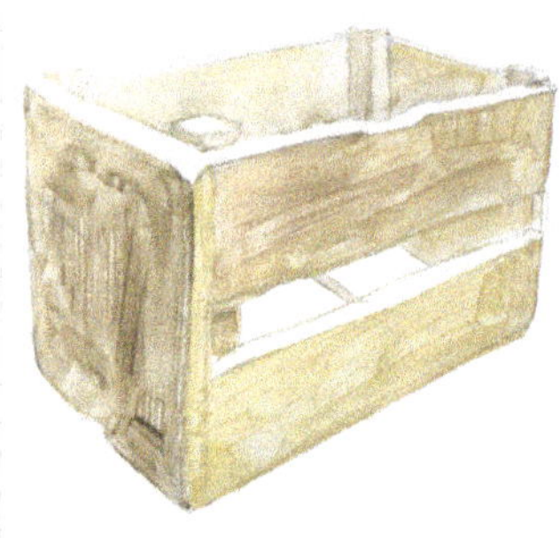

Start to paint medium tone colors with watered down acrylic washes.

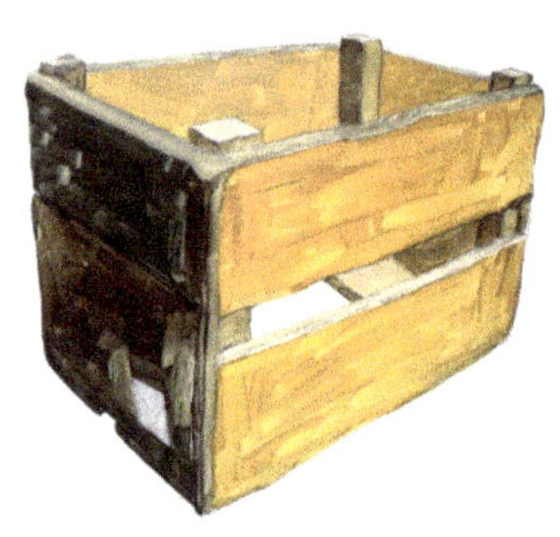

Place shadows using cool tones. Then place another layer of medium colors for the lighter areas. Use warmer colors for light areas and cooler colors for areas of shadow. Start to identify the general areas of shadows.

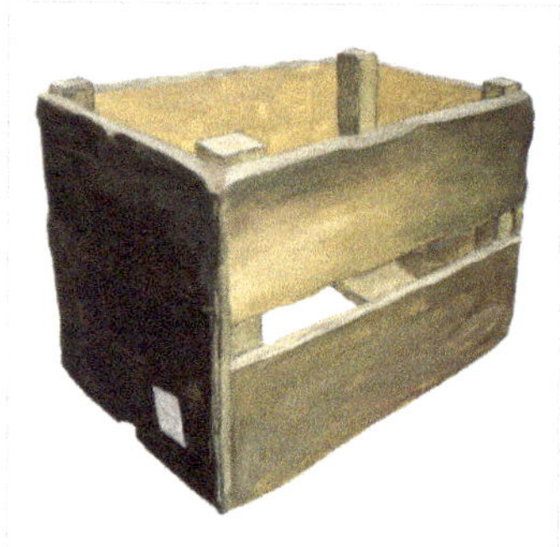

Make the details of the wooden textures. Pay attention to the overall volume. Smooth out the brushstrokes.

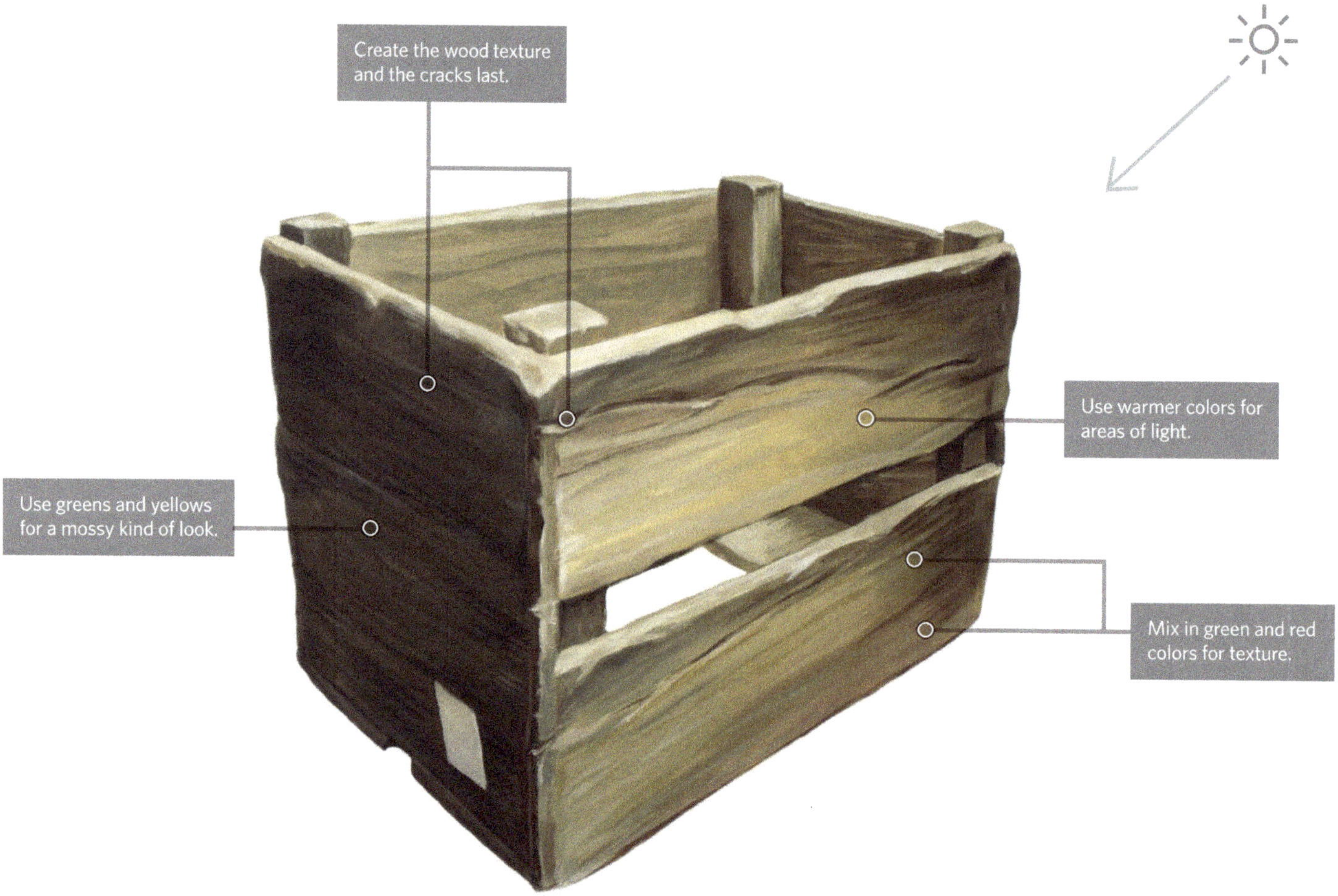

Create the wood texture and the cracks last.

Use warmer colors for areas of light.

Use greens and yellows for a mossy kind of look.

Mix in green and red colors for texture.

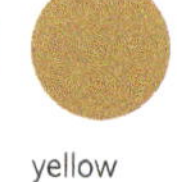

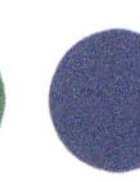
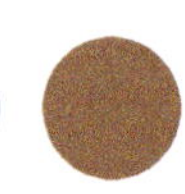

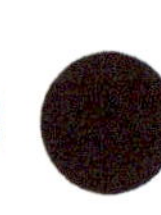

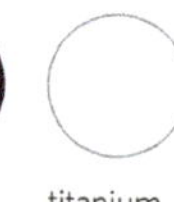

cadmium red, yellow ochre, permanent green, ultramarine blue, raw sienna, raw umber, burnt umber, mars black, titanium white

Now try painting the wooden crate yourself.

Now that you have practiced how to paint a wooden crate following a step-by-step tutorial, use the page on the right to try and paint from life. You can paint from the picture below or set up your own still life and try different variations of still life compositions.

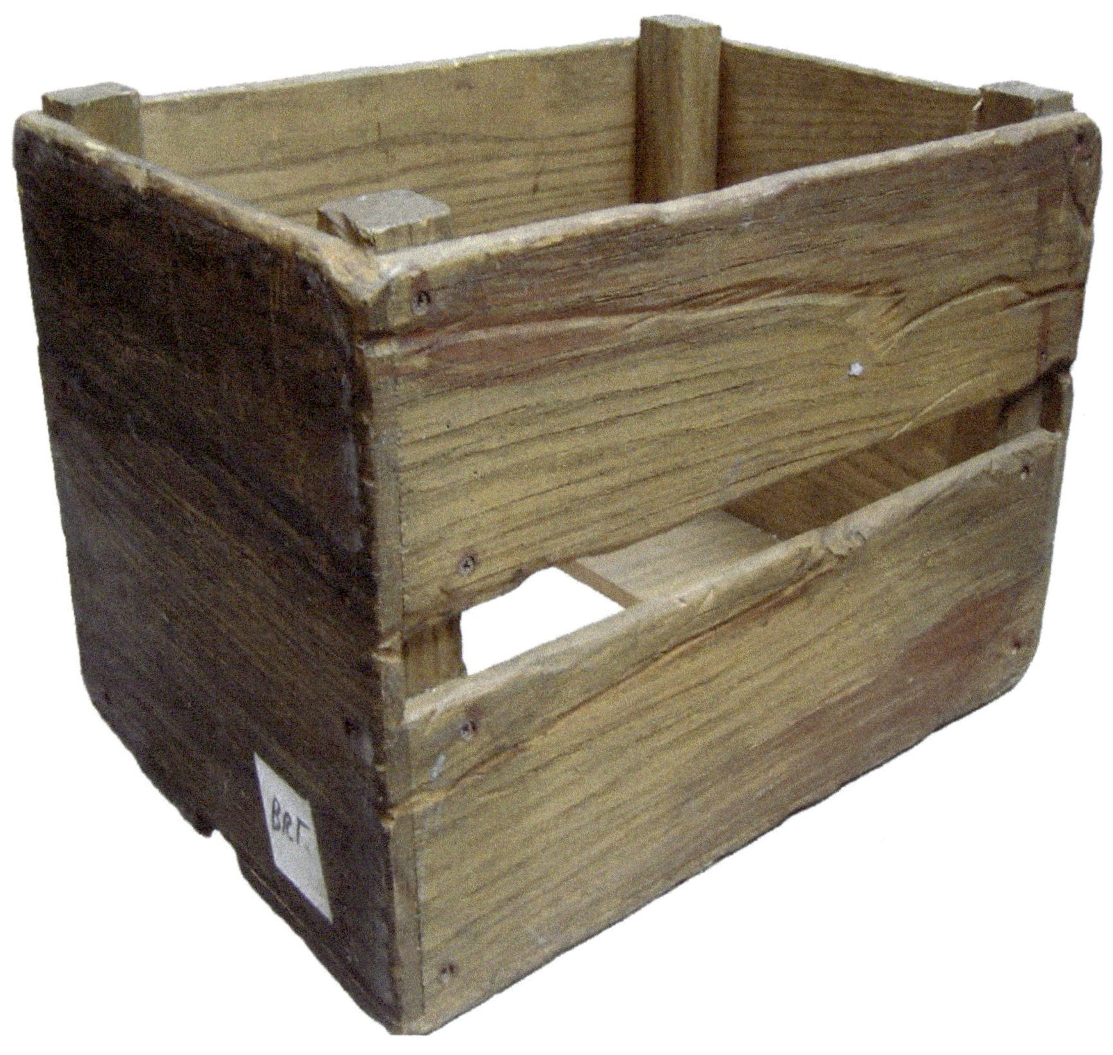

Now try painting the wooden crate yourself without the grid.

ABOUT OOGIE HAUS

Oogie Haus is an art foundation unique for its diverse artistic endeavors, including an emphasis in art education, art & design internship opportunities, and volunteer outreach programs. There have been several book publications as well, such as "Art College Admissions," an insightful guideline for students applying to art schools.

Besides being an educational resource, Oogie Haus functions dually as an art gallery and art dealership. Through its research, it seeks to contribute a bigger network for local and international artists simultaneously curating its unique voice in todays art world. For more information please visit www.oogiehaus.com

ABOUT THE AUTHOR

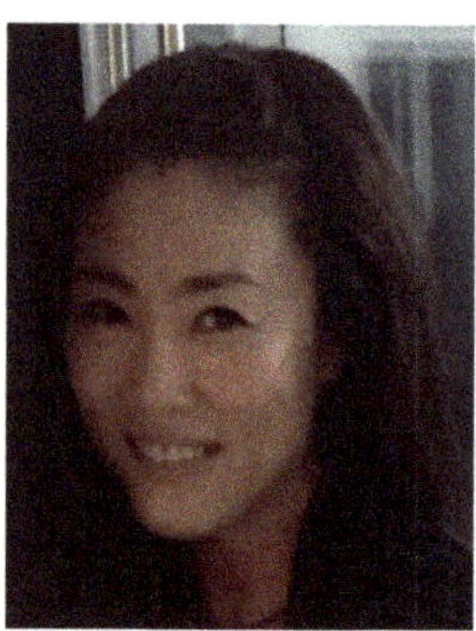

WOOK CHOI is an accomplished art dealer, education columnist, author, art educator, art gallerist, and art portfolio consultant who has guided over a thousand students to college admissions and scholarship success during the course of her 31-year teaching career.
She has received widespread recognition for her teaching methods from Mayor Michael Bloomberg; former First Lady Laura Bush; the New York Commissioner of Education, Richard P. Mills; US Congress member, Jerrold Nadler; the Alliance for Young Artists; YoungArts; and the Marie Walsh Sharpe Foundation. For more information, please visit www.wookchoi.com.

YOU CAN CONTINUE TO DEVELOP YOUR ARTISTIC SKILLS IN DIFFERENT MEDIA!

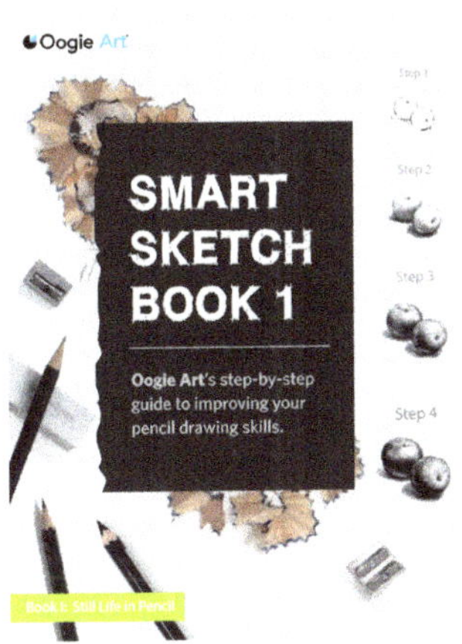

SMART SKETCHBOOK 1:
Still Life in Pencil

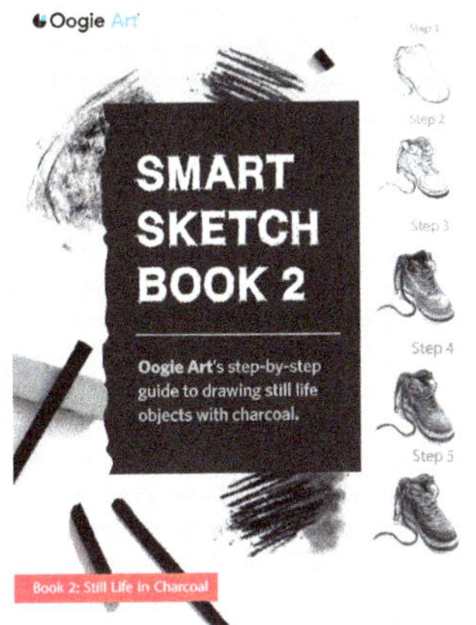

SMART SKETCHBOOK 2:
Still Life in Charcoal

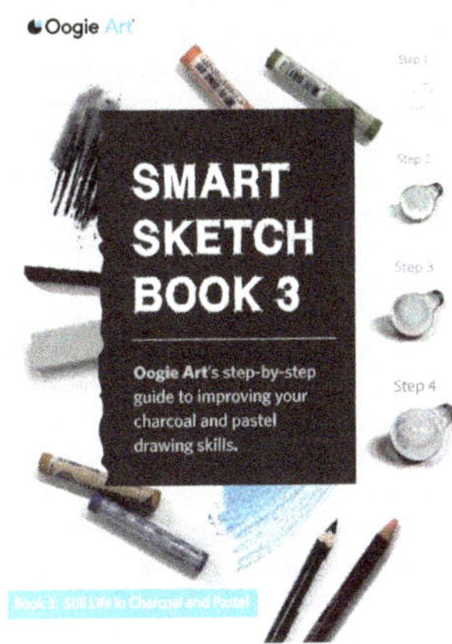

SMART SKETCHBOOK 3:
Still Life in Charcoal and Pastel

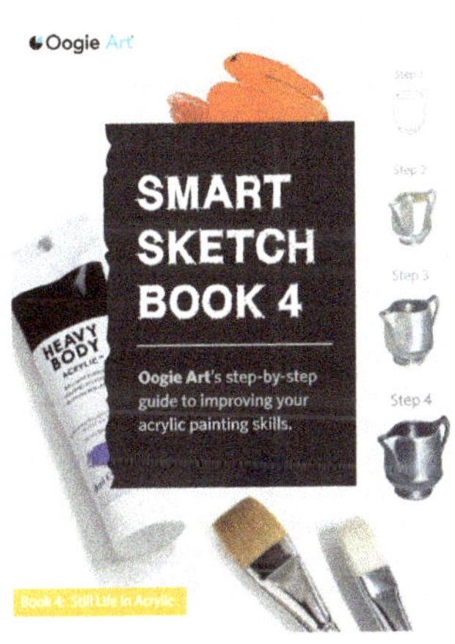

SMART SKETCHBOOK 4:
Still Life in Acrylic

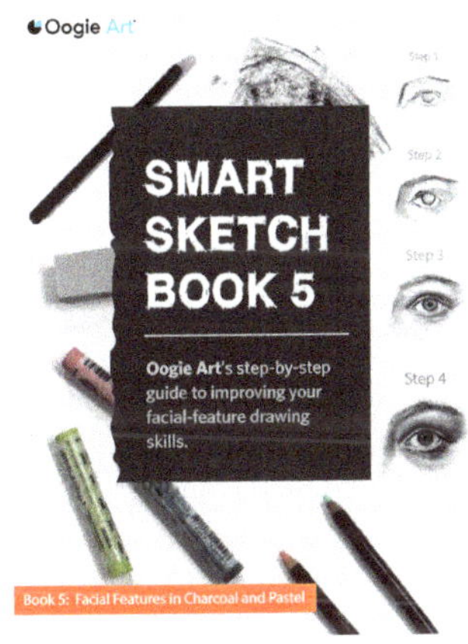

SMART SKETCHBOOK 5:
Facial Features in Charcoal and Pastel

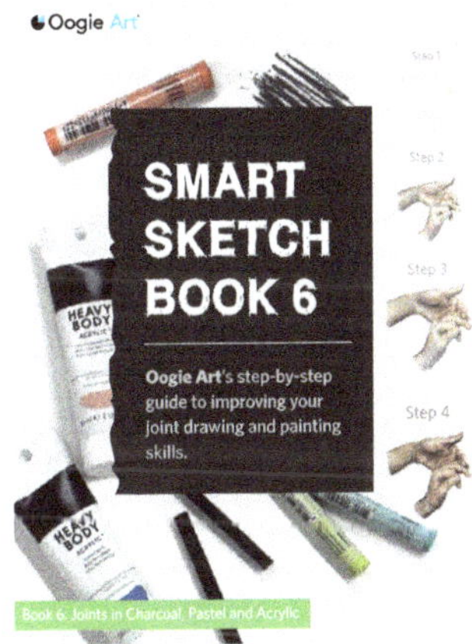

SMART SKETCHBOOK 6:
Joints in Charcoal, Pastel and Acrylic

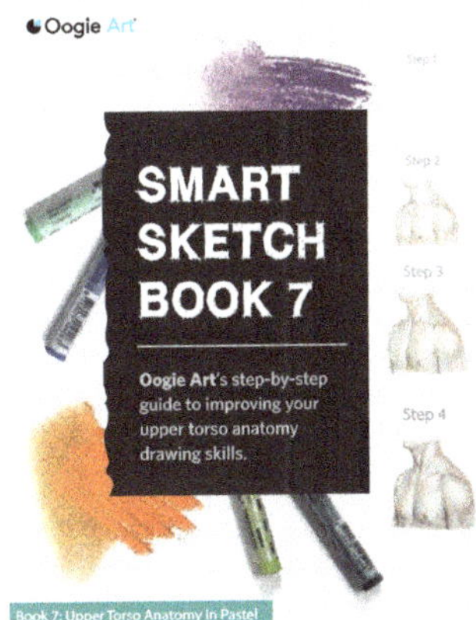

SMART SKETCHBOOK 7:
Upper Torso Anatomy in Pastel

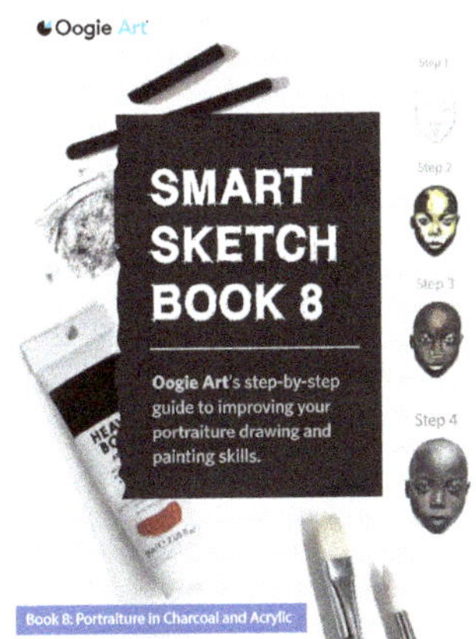

SMART SKETCHBOOK 8:
Portraiture in Charcoal and Acrylic

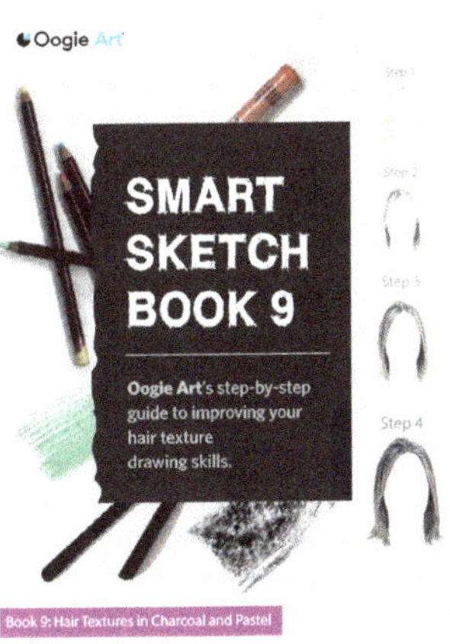

SMART SKETCHBOOK 9:
Hair Textures in Charcoal and Pastel

www.ingramcontent.com/pod-product-compliance
Ingram Content Group UK Ltd.
Pitfield, Milton Keynes, MK11 3LW, UK
UKHW062010290726
14090UKWH00022B/1483